The **SECRETS** of **SUCCESSFUL STUDENTS**

HOW TO BE **YOUR BEST** IN SCHOOL

D1173165

DANIEL G. AMEN, M.D.

MindWorksPress

A Division of Amen Clinics, Inc.

Published by MindWorks Press, Newport Beach, California.
A Division of Amen Clinics, Inc.

Amen Clinics, Inc.
www.amenclinics.com

Printed in the United States of America

Cover and Interior Design by Lightbourne

Interior Illustrations by Tom Muzzio

ISBN 1-886554-20-X

BOOKS AND PROGRAMS BY DANIEL AMEN

**MAKING A GOOD
BRAIN GREAT**
Random House, October 2005

**BRAIN AND
BEHAVIOR COURSE**
MindWorks Press, 2005

WHICH BRAIN DO YOU WANT
Video, MindWorks Press, 2005

**HOW TO GET OUT
OF YOUR OWN WAY**
MindWorks Press, 2005

**WHAT I LEARNED
FROM A PENGUIN**
MindWorks Press, 2005

**AMEN CLINIC BRAIN
SCIENCE TOOL BOX**
MindWorks Press, 2004

PREVENTING ALZHEIMER'S
with neurologist William R. Shankle,
Putnam, 2004

**HEALING ANXIETY
AND DEPRESSION**
with psychiatrist Lisa Routh, MD,
Putnam, 2003

**IMAGES OF HUMAN
BEHAVIOR: A Brain SPECT Atlas**
MindWorks Press, 2003

**NEW SKILLS FOR FRAZZLED
PARENTS**
MindWorks Press, 2003

**HEALING THE HARDWARE
OF THE SOUL**
Free Press, 2002

HEALING ADD
Putnam, 2001

**CHANGE YOUR BRAIN,
CHANGE YOUR LIFE**
Three Rivers Press, 1999,
New York Times Bestseller

**A TEENAGERS
GUIDE TO A.D.D.**
**(written with Antony Amen
and Sharon Johnson)**
MindWorks Press, 1995

**MINDCOACH: Teaching Kids To
Think Positive And Feel Good**
MindWorks Press, 1994

CONTENTS

INTRODUCTION

THIS BOOK WILL HELP STUDENTS ACHIEVE ACADEMIC EXCELLENCE from the sixth grade through graduate school, and beyond. It will also give teachers, instructors, and professors methods for helping students be more effective in their day-to-day studies. The principles in *The Secrets of Successful Students* apply to a broad spectrum of students, from students who are failing in school to outstanding students who want to become even more effective.

Academic failures are due to a multitude of problems, and *The Secrets of Successful Students* will systematically look at each major area of what I term "studenthood" and offer many practical solutions to the problems. Much like a tax cut stimulates a sluggish economy, this book gives students the emotional motivation necessary to help them change sluggish patterns.

This book is for a range of students. First, it helps the C student whose achievements are far below his or her capabilities. Many students think they are mediocre because they are simply not intelligence enough. In truth, it is their knowledge of *how* to learn that is inadequate, not their ability *to* learn. I have seen average students become consistent B and even A students after applying the techniques in this book.

This book will help outstanding students as well. These students often achieve academically because they use massive assault tactics when they study, focusing virtually all of their time and energy on scholastic success. By doing so, they often neglect other areas of their lives. This book helps those students direct their efforts and economize their time, leaving room for other pursuits and personal development.

The Secrets of Successful Students is also for the working person who is either going back to school after a long absence or taking job-related training. It is estimated that almost one-quarter of the adult population in the U.S. is enrolled in some form of regular study, and that people in skilled professions or trades require retraining every five to six years to keep abreast of new developments in their fields. These people usually have more outside responsibilities than the typical college student and therefore less time to devote to their studies. **They** have a pressing need to be frugal with their time, and in order to accomplish their goals, they need to use the best study methods available.

In short, this book is for anyone who wants to learn anything faster, better, and more effectively. Its principles are practical and easy to use in almost any learning situation.

Reading, Studying, and Interpersonal Skills

Reading, studying, and relational skills are three essential components for every student's success. Unfortunately, reading skills are not routinely taught past junior high school, unless a student is reading at a level far below his or her classmates. Even the "normal" range of reading ability is far below the potential of most students; this usually handicaps them in college and graduate school. Being able to read swiftly and with adequate comprehension is essential to education. This book shows you how to improve your reading skills and suggests techniques to help you achieve greater speed and comprehension.

Study skills are neglected even more than reading skills. I remember having basic reading classes in grammar school but **never having a formal** class on how to study, one of the most basic of all educational skills. Again, these courses are available but are usually reserved for failing or marginal students. Your skill in studying, not your intelligence quotient, often determines how well you will do in school. A significant portion of this book is devoted to improving your study skills.

Interpersonal skills are virtually ignored in the classroom! It is the rare teacher or classmate who, when confronted **with** unacceptable behavior, tries to understand the person's need to act that way. Usually the person is labeled "character deficient" and the behavior is taken as an **affront**. Interpersonal skills have much to do with performance because we live in a relational world. You can be an academic wizard, but if you cannot relate **well** to your teachers and peers, you will suffer as a student! *The Secrets of Successful Students* is a relational book. It contains a wealth of references to the value of human interactions in learning and many suggestions for improving these interactions. The relational skills you learn in this book will even enable you to obtain higher grades!

Grades

I have heard it said many times that grades are not important. However, having served on both college and medical school admissions committees, I know that grades are important!

Grades are often the deciding factor on whether a person will be allowed to continue working toward his or her academic or professional goals! It is to **your** advantage to enhance your academic or professional options by acquiring the practical knowledge you need and a good grade point average. This book will help you achieve both.

It has also been said that grades do not necessarily reflect a person's knowledge and should have no effect on a person's self-esteem, or academic ranking, or professional success. Even though this statement contains an element of truth, it does not have much practical value. A steady stream of "hooks," or C's, does not enhance self-esteem! If you know a lot but cannot convey it on a test or in a class-room situation, what value does it have for you in achieving your academic or professional goals?

How is *The Secrets of Successful Students* Different?

Many books have been written on how to study. What makes this one different? First, it is not just a book on how to study—it is much more! It is a handbook on how to benefit from being a student, how to profit personally by excelling as a student, and how to do both of these without jeopardizing other areas of your life.

Second, several sections of this book are especially unique. They include the chapters on change and motivation (1), preparation (2), class skills (7), studying with a partner (9), and approaching teachers (10).

Third, I have personally tested and proved the effectiveness of every method or suggestion outlined in this book. I am not going to tell you what other people think. I am going to tell you what I know works!

Fourth, it is written by someone who studies human behavior for a living and who is close enough to his own academic career to know what can realistically be expected of students. In addition, using the principles in this book, I made the transition from being an average student to excelling in school. In grammar school and high school I floundered in mediocrity, struggling to get C's and some B's. I didn't have the right learning tools. In college, however, I decided to become a medical doctor and realized that if I didn't change my approach to school I would never be able to **achieve** my goals. **I became a student by learning how to be a student**. This book is about what I learned. In college I graduated "summa cum laude" with a 3.93 grade point average (on a 4.0 scale), and in medical school I graduated second in my class, only behind my study partner. In my last two years of medical school, I taught a seminar to first-year medical students on "how to do medical school."

This book is not meant to be an exhaustive textbook on how to excel in all subjects. It is written as therapy for students' souls—as a concise source of inspiration, full of practical ideas. You can read it quickly and reap its benefits immediately. Even though this book is relatively short, its scope is broad, touching on everything from underlining techniques to getting a date in class. Its principles apply to students and educators in any discipline from high school to graduate school, and beyond. Its applications are endless!

The Bottom Line

The bottom line is the payoff you can expect from the time and money you have invested in this book. Learn how to:

1. Quickly identify bad study habits and replace them with ones that get results

2. Prepare for classes, making them worthwhile, but decreasing overall study time

3. Get the overall big picture and see how it relates to a solid foundation for learning

4. Organize yourself and your time

5. Understand the different study methods and choose the ones that are best for you

6. Get the most from lectures and note taking

7. Memorize faster and remember longer

8. Pick a great study partner and understand why it is crucial for you to have one;

9. Develop relationships with teachers and make full use of them as valuable resources in your education

10. Skillfully prepare for and take exams

11. Improve your writing and speaking skills

Overall, this book shows you how to "work smarter, not harder," so that you no longer waste time on aimless study and instead acquire more knowledge with less effort. You will develop skills that serve you well during school and throughout your life as you continue to learn. Of course, as you master these skills, your grades will reflect the changes.

With Your Bus Ticket in Hand

In *The Great Divorce*, C.S. Lewis described an intense bus ride from hell toward heaven. He makes it very clear in the book that the characters' actions and attitudes were responsible for their disadvantageous situation. Only after choosing to get on the bus and ride on the path toward change, did they avail themselves of the opportunity to improve their circumstances. By purchasing this book, you have obtained your bus ticket for a more satisfying "studenthood." Now, get on the bus and ride to more effective methods of study and better grades, making sure you enjoy yourself along the way!

CHAPTER ONE

CHANGING HABITS:

AVOIDING THE GRASSHOPPER MENTALITY

I F YOU PLACE A GRASSHOPPER IN A JAR WITH A LID,
you can learn a powerful lesson about human behavior.
Grasshoppers in this kind of captivity behave as many people do throughout their lives. At first, the imprisoned
grasshopper tries desperately to escape from the jar, using his
powerful hind legs to launch his body up against the lid. He
tries and tries, and then he tries again. Initially, he is very per-
sistent. He may try to get out of his trap for several hours.
When he finally stops, however, his trying days are over. He
will never again try to escape from the jar by jumping. You
could take the lid off of the jar and have a pet grasshopper for
life. Once a grasshopper believes that he cannot change his situation, that's it. He stops trying.

In a similar way, once an elephant learns something, it
stays with him for life. Many circus elephants are trained as
babies to stay in one place by placing a strong chain around
one ankle. Like the grasshoppers, they initially struggle and
struggle to get free until they cannot struggle any more. Once

they stop the struggling they will never again try to break loose from something holding them by the ankle. Powerful adult elephants can be held in place by just a thin rope around one of their legs. It has been reported that elephants have burned to death in circus fires when the huge beasts were tethered only by small, easily broken ropes around their legs.

It is easy to see the parallel between grasshoppers, elephants, and people (students) who are stuck in negative behavior patterns: Once they believe they are defeated, that they cannot do things to change their situation, they stop **trying. They** give up. Even if the lid is removed from their traps, it doesn't occur to them to leave. Even if success or happiness is within their grasp, they are unable to reach **out** and grab it. They remain stuck.

You are not a grasshopper, or an elephant, or any other lower life form for that matter. You are a human being, the highest form of life form ever known. You are separated from the lower life forms by your ability to think, your ability to reason, and most importantly, your ability to adapt and change as your environment dictates. Adaptability is the reason human beings, despite being smaller and weaker than many animal species, have come to rule the world. You are not a grasshopper; you are able to change old ways if you think about them and develop a plan for progress.

Changing poor study habits is the first step toward becoming an effective student. The process of change involves five things: motivation, attitude, tools, perseverance, and setting yourself up to win.

Motivation

Motivation is that which moves a person. What moves you? Are you studying to improve yourself or to fulfill future goals?

Are you studying to impress your family or friends, or are you unsure of the reasons for **your** work? The first principle of change is to understand why you need to do it. Are you a high school student who wants to go to a prestigious university? Are you the sophomore **pre-med** student who needs an A in organic chemistry or the junior **psychology** major who needs to finish with very good grades to have a chance at a competitive graduate school? Are you the **business** student who wants to prepare the best possible resume for job interviews? Or are you the student who just wants to get better grades and learn more while expending less energy? Write down **your** reason(s) for wanting to become a better student. See what motivates you, and be sure that your motives are clear and decisive. You will be more likely to perform at your peak if you have insight into what fuels your engine.

Never forget that motivation is your business! In higher educations you will encounter very little coaxing or pleading to motivate you. Take responsibility for your inspiration and organize your goals into a force that will start your metamorphosis from the inefficient plodder to the champion student!

Attitude

Your attitude toward your work will either be a motivating strength or a constant drag on your energy. Approach your studies with the idea of gaining the most that you can; it is the only rational way to spend your time. If you are constantly looking beyond what you are studying, or see it as meaningless, you will be irritated by the experience and resent the time it takes to reach your goal. If you concentrate on getting the most from each class you will find that time will not be a problem for you.

During this time of transition to better study habits, you must assume an attitude of confidence. Believing in your ability to achieve is paramount to success. One of the best ways to enhance self-confidence is to surround yourself with people who believe in your abilities and who build you up. Friends, family, and professors who are on your "team" or who are rooting for you make life a joy. Stay away from people who are constantly putting you down, telling you that the field of your choice is too competitive, or that you are not smart enough to succeed. During my sophomore year in college, after I had decided to go to medical school, my speech teacher told me her younger brother did not get into medical school, even though he was twice as smart as I. In other words, I didn't have a chance. Needless to say, I quickly cut off most of my communication with her because I might have believed her if I had listened long enough!

On the other hand, as I talked to my father about the medical school adventure, he told me that I could do anything I set my mind to. He was right, you know. Of course, I had setbacks like everyone else. I remember times when I would get emotionally down about the pressures or workload at school. My dad would grab the hair on the back of my head (he would grab it harder when it was a little long), and he would say, "Boy, you are going to make it." Then he would give me a swift kick in the part of the anatomy that is marked "please place all swift kicks here" and tell me to straighten up. Thank God I had his confidence to lean on when mine was weak. Where would I be now if I had listened to those people who did not believe in me? I hate to think of it. So go forward with confidence and surround yourself with people who see your potential and support it.

Tools

Next, get the proper tools. Where would the surgeon be without his scalpel and retractors? This book gives you the necessary tools for study and offers many practical aids for sharpening those tools. Any good grocery store owner knows his inventory, and so should you. Take a few min-

utes to write out five weaknesses and five strengths you have, regarding your study skills. If you know your strengths and weaknesses, then you will be able to chose and use the right tools to improve your weak areas and build on the strong ones.

Practice and review your study skills often. Studying is not instinctive or automatic. It is more like kissing. Do you remember your first kisses? I would have starved if I had to make a living at the kissing booth at the fair! But as the years progressed, I became quite adept. So it is with studying. Practice and review are the best ways to keep your skill level at its peak.

Perseverance

In order to change bad study habits or patterns, you must develop perseverance. Most people never reach their full potential because they simply don't keep trying. You need to understand two concepts before you can make perseverance work for you: 1.) You must count the cost ahead of time and 2.) You will experience a certain amount of pain before you reach your goal.

Jesus said, "Suppose one of you wants to build a tower. Will he not first sit down and estimate the cost to see if he has enough money to complete it? For if he lays the foundations and is not able to finish it, everyone who sees it will ridicule him, saying, 'This fellow began to build and was not able to finish.'

Or suppose a king is about to go to war against another king. Will he not first sit down and consider whether he is able, with ten thousand men, to oppose the one coming against him with twenty thousand? If he is not able, he will send a delegation while the other is still a long way off and will ask for terms of peace."

In order to persevere, you must know what you are up against. If you count the cost of the goals you are pursuing, you will be less likely to start something that you will later drop.

Pain also plays a role in learning perseverance. I believe American society maintains the assumption that all pain is

bad. I find, however, that all pain is not bad and that in many instances pain is a natural and necessary ingredient for personal growth. Growth and change both involve pain. There were many nights when my son was small that he awakened in the night, moaning from the pain in his legs. As my wife or I massaged his little legs or placed a cool, wet cloth on them, the growing pains would subside. Antony learned to accept the pain of physical growth because it fit into his desire to be as tall as his grandfather, who is six feet, four inches.

There is pain in any learning situation. You will experience the pain of hard work and long nights, studying when your friends are playing, postponing material or social goals for academic ones, and even doing poorly on an exam after studying hard for it because the teacher asked "off the wall" questions. Prepare yourself for the pain and accept its place in your personal life and in your study life. It will help you persevere and develop to your full potential. Accept this and you will not revert to old habits or drop out when the going gets rough.

Set Yourself Up to Win

Finally, you must set yourself up to win. Do this by starting slowly, at a pace that is easy to handle. If you have not been to school for ten years, do not expect to successfully take twenty-four college credits a semester. If this is your first semester in college, do not overexert yourself or you may quickly run out of energy. Just as a good runner builds up muscle slowly, so should you build up your academic stamina the same way. If you start too fast, you will end up like the runner who tries to run five miles after a two-year layoff. He will have torn muscles. You will have a shattered ego.

You also need to confidently take well-planned risks. The only way to gain that confidence is by taking risks and winning at them most of the time. I have heard many students say that they wanted to be a doctor, lawyer, journalist, or engineer, but they did not have the smarts for it. That is usually not true. If you follow the principles in this book and take a systematic approach to study and to your career goals, you can push yourself to achieve great academic heights, even those you feel are beyond your grasp. No one ever accomplished anything worthwhile however, without risking time, money, and especially pride.

To set yourself up to win, also give yourself liberal doses of positive, reinforcing experiences. Success breeds success! Do your best in the beginning of each class. You will feel good about your accomplishments, and you will want to experience that feeling again. This will spur you on. If you don't do your best right from the beginning of semester, you will be continually behind and feel inadequate. Since no one likes to feel that way, you may drop out to rid yourself of the feeling.

If you come to class prepared, however, you will be able to participate and be encouraged to prepare more often. This is an invaluable lesson in life. Set yourself up to win and you will win! Set yourself up to lose and you will lose. It's that simple.

"The Big Picture" of Changing Habits

1. Find out what motivates you to study better and decide to change bad study habits.

2. Use you attitude to fuel change while you surround yourself with people who believe in your potential.

3. Gather the proper tools for change

4. Persevere, counting the cost of your endeavors beforehand and accepting the pain that is a natural part of that change and growth.

5. Set yourself up to succeed by starting at a reasonable pace and taking well-planned risks. Give yourself positive, reinforcing experiences. This is the key to having the confidence of a winner.

CHAPTER TWO

IN THE BEGINNING:

PREPARATION FOR LEARNING

IN THE BEGINNING GOD CREATED MAN. RIGHT? No, that is wrong. In the beginning God created the heavens and the earth. Then he proceeded to create the day and the night, the sun, the moon and the stars, the land and the sea, the forests and the gardens, the fish, the birds and the mammals, etc. He took into account all that was necessary and prepared extensively for his ultimate purpose—the creation of man. Maybe he took into account more than was necessary. Who needs leeches and stink bugs?

Whether or not you accept the above description of the history of our genesis is not the point. What is important is that preparation is paramount to accomplishment. With a solid foundation, goals become achievable; without it—impossible.

Start at the Beginning with Preparation

So where do you start? Where else but at the beginning. If you want to study writing, you need to learn grammar and vocabulary. If you want to enter the business world, you need to learn basic mathematics and accounting skills. If you want to be a physician, you should start with basic chemistry and physics. And if you want to be a minister, begin with the Bible and learn public speaking techniques.

To carry this point even further, it is necessary to start at the beginning of the beginning. This may sound redundant, but this simple principle will save you many hours of frustration and stress. In chemistry, for example, it is essential to know that gold is a metal before you can possible understand how it reacts to heat. One must know the functions of nouns and verbs before putting together sentences for a short story. It is certainly essential in psychology or medicine to understand what is normal, before you can comprehend what is abnormal.

So how does this translate into good study habits? First, make sure you take the adequate prerequisites for any course you want to take. I remember my first week of general chemistry in college. I was so lost that I thought I was in the wrong room, taking Russian language class. I had taken the prerequisite chemistry class in high school, but barely squeaked by with a C. The smartest thing I did for my career was drop the class in general chemistry and take a beginning chemistry course. That "dumbbell" class gave me the solid foundation and adequate preparation I needed for all of my future encounters with chemistry.

Good preparation may delay your plans by a few months, but inadequate preparation is the major reason students drop out of tough programs. So be a good scout and "Be Prepared" for what you are about to encounter.

Reading Skills

Reading skills are basic to a successful academic career, regardless of your discipline. I will not dwell on the mechanics of good reading, because most high schools and colleges offer elective courses in reading skills, which I highly recommend if you need them. I will, however, offer a few simple observations on reading. First, reading for pleasure and reading for study are two completely different animals. One usually takes on the feeling of a warm, cuddly puppy, while the other often resembles a vile cockroach!

When reading to learn, always keep a dictionary nearby to look up new words. This habit will rapidly build your vocabulary and increase your knowledge of any subject.

Also make sure you use the study aids provided in most textbooks. These include the Table of Contents, charts, graphs, illustrations, italicized words, and above all, the summary statements and study guides at the end of each chapter.

Try to enjoy what you are reading and consider its value to you. I know that this is not always possible, and I have spent more time than I care to admit reading words that were put together purposely to confuse and torment me. Again, by using end-of-chapter reviews, you can maintain a sense of the "the big picture" and see its value. This makes it easier to wade through the toughest material.

Read with a purpose and know ahead of time what you want to accomplish when you have finished a section. It is good to keep a running tab of where you are and where you are heading—not a bad principle in life, either! If you follow a plan, you will waste less time, and unproductive time is what you want to completely eliminate.

When you are reading and begin to feel lost, ask yourself, "When did I first feel lost?" Then go back to that point and begin again until you understand. If you continue to read without understanding, you will either never learn the material, or you will struggle with it much longer than necessary. The sooner you go back, when lost, the better it will be for you, your spouse, your children, your friends, your foes, and your dog, because you will be less irritable. A very important statement is repeated several times in the book of Genesis. At the end of each day in creation, God said, "and it was good." Make sure that you can say the same thing after each section you study: "It is good. I understand it." If you find yourself saying, "It is good, but I never meant to be studying Greek" start over at the beginning of your lesson until you feel comfortable with the material.

As you have probably already noticed, most class material pyramids, that is, it builds upon a base of knowledge. That is why I want to emphasize the importance of reading the preface, introduction, and introductory chapters of textbooks. Do not skip them. They give you valuable information that is overlooked by most students. These sections and chapters give you invaluable information on the following: how to use the textbook efficiently; how to study the subject; the unique features of the book; why the subject is important; and interesting information about the authors to help make the subject matter less impersonal and more relevant. Reading these portions of the text familiarizes you with the task ahead. It also gives you an early opportunity to return the book and drop out of the class if it is not what you expected or wanted. For example, when I was a junior in college, I enrolled in a biochemistry course that I thought would be helpful in my medical education. After reading the preface, introduction, and first two chapters of the text, I quickly found that I did not want to put myself through that kind of pain twice, since I had to take a similar class in medical school. I dropped the class and took a course on death and dying, which, although more morbid, was less painful and certainly more interesting.

The last observation on reading involves distractions and how to avoid them. Unless you are Pope John Paul II, who, it is rumored, can read a book and hold a high level interview at the same time, it is very difficult to concentrate well on more than one thing at a time. You need your own private haven for the task of effective studying. Now we must ask, "What sort of surroundings help make study sessions more efficient?"

The Study Environment

Most of what is said here involves common sense. First, find a place that is comfortable and quiet. Comfort is important because if you feel good physically you will be able to study longer. Quiet, because you are not the Pope! Unless you have insomnia, do not study on your bed. The message you are sending your brain when read lying down is the opposite of your purpose. (Unless, of course, you happen to be taking a class on the interpretation of dreams.)

Try to keep your study place well ventilated and as cool as you can comfortably tolerate. This will help keep away sleepy images of warm afternoons by the lake.

Make sure you have good lighting that shines over the opposite shoulder of your writing arm. This will diminish shadows while you read and take notes. Also make sure you can easily adjust the light to reduce the glare from glossy textbook pages. Choose a chair that is comfortable, but not to the extent of encouraging you to fantasize that it is a first-class seat aboard a plane bound for Honolulu.

Make your desk, table, or study area large enough to give you plenty of room to spread out, so you do not feel cluttered. Only the material you are studying should be out on your workspace. All other distractions should be out of sight. For example, do not study next to the telephone and keep newspapers, magazines, old correspondence, and the TV out of reach.

There are varying opinions on the use of the radio during study time. My experience has been that soft, instrumental music may enhance study sessions. It seems obvious, however, that punk rock will *not* help you assimilate the details of fine art in the Baroque period!

Study Breaks and Aids

The need for breaks during study sessions varies greatly from person to person. However, if the bag boy at the Safeway down the street gets ten minutes every two hours, then you should take at least that much time, preferably ten minutes every hour, with limbering exercises or stretches every twenty minutes. There is good reason why psychiatrists see patients for only fifty minutes at a time. So take the hint and give yourself a break.

A quick word about study aids. Be prepared. If you are going to need something during the study session, get it beforehand so that you can work efficiently and use break times only to relax and rejuvenate, not run around grabbing supplies and resources.

"The Big Picture" In the Beginning

Preparation is paramount to accomplishment.

1. Start at the beginning of the beginning and solidify your academic foundation before you move ahead.

2. Polish your reading skills by using the dictionary and comprehension aids. See the value in what you read and have a purpose when reading by following a plan. Read the introductory material of your texts. Avoid distractions.

3. Maintain a comfortable and quiet study environment by keeping the room cool and by having good light, a comfortable chair, and enough space to work. Remember to keep distractions out of sight. Soft music is better than hard rock.

4. Take breaks.

CHAPTER THREE

THE BIG PICTURE:

FROM GENERALIZATIONS TO SPECIFICS

WHEN I BEGAN TUTORING IN MY SOPHOMORE year of college, I was amazed to discover that some of my students could remember facts I had never even heard. The only reason, it seemed to me, that I was the tutor and they were the tutees, was that I knew where the facts belonged and could put them into a rational sequence. For them, many facts were hanging like leaves without branches to support them.

If I was amazed in college, I was astounded in medical school to find a very similar situation. You would think medical students have it all together when it comes to good study habits and knowing the importance of getting "the big picture" before knowing the details. To my shock, I found the study skills of many medical students on a par with neurotic monkeys who learn information only after numerous repetitions. It is true that the average intelligence of the medical students with whom I had contact was quite high, and that is how they achieved their success. But my soul ached for the literally thousands of hours these students wasted in circular, repetitive, and unprofitable study. I wonder what great discoveries could have been made if they had those hours back, but as the Apostle Paul said, "Forgetting that which is behind and straining toward what is ahead, I press on toward the high mark." And that, is part of what this book is all about, getting high marks.

I think getting the big picture in a subject is the first step in mastering it, and a step that many students omit. Now, I know many of you are expecting me to tell you that you are having trouble seeing the forest because of the trees, which is most likely the case. As you know, if you do not realize that you are in a forest, it is very easy to get lost in the maze of trees and foliage that surround you. If, however, you do know where you are and what you are doing there, the forest can be a wonderful place.

Another analogy, that of a trip I once made, is useful in driving this point home (or as happened to me, drive me further from home.) I was traveling with my wife from California to Oklahoma. We had made this trip four or five times before, always driving from Los Angeles, to Needles, to Flagstaff, etc. At that particular time, however, I was just becoming a junior in medical school and must have felt the extraordinary powers of my position in life, when I decided that there must be a quicker way to Flagstaff than through Needles. After all, what did the Auto Club know (having mapped out the trip) that a third-year medical student did not?

As I eyed the map, I saw a shortcut from Blythe, California, to Flagstaff, Arizona, saving us about two inches on the map. The only short cut was only a single red line, instead of a double green one, and it had several curves in it. So against my wife's objection, we headed for the short cut at about nine-thirty at night, expecting to arrive in Flagstaff about two o'clock in the morning. As you have probably realized by now, we spent the next ten hours negotiating the sharpest curves and steepest mountain grades that Arizona has to offer.

I certainly missed the big picture (which my wife did not let me forget for the next eleven hundred miles) because I did not have an accurate, overall plan or outline for our trip. It would have been simple to check the map key to see what a single red line meant or to trust the experts who help plan such trips. But determination to make one's own way without the proper preparation, guideposts, or even a reasonable scheme can be very counter-productive.

The practical applications of this big-picture principle are many and apply in almost every situation in which the understanding of principles and concepts is necessary. Even in a dating situation, it is advantageous to ask the other person for a date and have him or her accept before attending to all the details, i.e., buying tickets, making reservations, etc. For without the big picture, which in this case is the date, you really have nothing at all.

In writing, the big picture means having an outline of your thoughts before you begin putting them on paper. Such a road map makes it possible to know where you are going. In public speaking, it is essential to know where you want to take your audience. It is certainly much simpler, in writing a paper or a speech, to start with general ideas and integrate specifics, instead of beginning with isolated details and trying to connect them in a logical form.

An idea is also easier to understand if you know its context. For example, look at some instances in the development of personality. If you rationally look at the behavior of four years olds, you notice that they have many psychotic traits. They are frequently found talking to themselves or their invisible friends. They have many delusions of grandeur, thinking that they are the fictitious characters they see on TV or read about in books. They also think they could run the house and marry mommy if only daddy would go away! These four year olds seem to be constantly hallucinating, screaming that bears are in their bathrooms, or that incredibly large creatures, monsters, whatchamacallits, or whatever are under their beds. If this information on four year-olds were not viewed in relation to the context or big picture of their development, our state mental hospitals would look like nursery schools.

In medical school, you will painfully hang yourself on the trees if you do not see the forest for what it is. In the first year of medical school alone, freshmen learn 25,000 new words; in the second year they learn an additional 25,000 words. If they do not have a system for learning new words and putting them into their proper context or big picture, their brains will undoubtedly go on strike and refuse to process anything but confusion and schizophrenic thoughts. However, if they learn the suffixes, prefixes, and common denominators of root words, their task becomes tolerable.

Before you get discouraged with the details, know "the big picture" of your subject matter. Also know where you have been and where you are going. If you feel lost in the details, simply stop, look for the main idea, then work your way down to the specifics. For example, if you are studying American history and need to know what specific events happened in 1932, your task will be made simpler if you first understand the events of major importance that preceded and followed 1932.

It has been said that we remember only 10 to 15 percent of what we learn in high school and college, and that we use less than one half of that. Unfortunately, medical school is the same way. Most of us are lucky if we retain the big picture. However, if you have never cultivated the big picture in your academic career, then you won't have much to show for your work, except a degree.

You might take some consolation in this comment from the dean of my medical school: "In ten years, 80 percent of what you learned in medical school will be obsolete (comforting thought). You are here not only to learn certain medical subjects, but more importantly to learn a lifelong method of learning and problem solving." It has been my experience that having a solid foundation and being constantly aware of the big picture is more than half of the battle.

At this point many of you might be saying to yourselves, "It would be nice to remember this stuff after graduation, but I'm worried about just getting through next Tuesday. 'The big picture' is fine, but you never had Dr. Wilson, whose test next week will question me on the number of electrons of hydrogen in a milliliter of tsetse fly saliva." Believe me, I have had my share of those teachers who thought that their academic corners were the only important ones. Not to worry, the big-picture approach works effectively even as you pursue the pickiest of details. If you schedule yourself and your study time, you will have the time to get "the big picture" of even the pickiest detail. But if you start with the details, you will never have the time to get the big picture.

There was one particular student in my medical school class who was infamous for having the details without the corresponding concepts. He often made us nervous because of the amount of time he studied and the volume of facts that he knew. But because the big picture usually escaped him, he had trouble with many tests. He was often outraged when those who knew only "the big picture" did better than he did.

Once his roommate (who was in charge of extracurricular partying) got a 98 percent on a histology laboratory exam after studying only two hours. His own grade, however, was in the seventies after studying more than ten hours. When he heard the test scores he fell to his knees and cried out about the injustice of it all. I agree, if you are going to spend the time, you should be rewarded for you effort. Just keep in mind that, more often than not, having the big picture means getting the bigger rewards.

"The Big Picture" of "The Big Picture"

1. Start with generalities and then work toward the specifics.

2. Keep the big picture of what you are doing constantly in front of you.

3. The big picture is what you will remember. It is your key to understanding the details.

CHAPTER FOUR

THE ORGANIZATION:

ORGANIZING YOUR CLASSES,
YOUR TIME, AND YOURSELF

THE MAJOR REASON THAT UNDERWORLD CRIME has been so phenomenally successful in this country is spelled out in a name often given to it: The Organization. The massive hierarchical web of godfathers, bosses, hit men, front men, and the rest would be very ineffective if there was not an extensive, internal organizational structure to their madness.

Organization like discipline is, to many students, a bad word. Both of these principles, however, can make your study life easier and much more profitable. Author Scott Peck, M.D., writes about discipline in his book *The Road Less Traveled.* I feel his words are also pertinent to the idea of organization. "Discipline," he says, "is the basic set of tools we require to solve life's problems. Without discipline (organization) we can solve nothing. With only some discipline (organization) we can solve only some problems. With total discipline (organization) we can solve all problems."

Now I know that many of you are thinking that many of the world's great discoveries happened by chance or fluke experiences. So why do you need to be organized or have so much discipline? I will let John Mackay, former football coach of the national champion USC Trojans, answer that one. He said, "If you are prepared for luck, you can take advantage of it. If you are not, then it will usually pass you by."

Most people think that when Sir Alexander Fleming discovered penicillin in 1928 at St. Mary's Hospital in London, it was a freak accident. It is true that by chance he noticed a mold contaminant on a culture plate of staphylococci, which had resulted in a killing zone of the bacteria. But without his previous foundation in microbiology, the organization of his laboratory, his time, and his discipline to follow through on his discovery, that chance accident might have gone unnoticed for fifty more years! In fact, that accident of nature must have occurred many times before, but no one was sufficiently prepared to discover it.

Is Your Time on Schedule?

So how do you begin putting together an organizational structure that will increase your effectiveness and even reduce your study time? First, you need to organize the time you have. Time can be a trusted ally or, as is usually the case, a harassing enemy. Before you can organize your time, you need to have an idea of how you spend your 1,440 minutes a day. The best way to do that is to follow yourself around for a week, taking stock of what you do and how much time you spend doing it. Take a large sheet of paper and divide it into columns representing your major activities, such as sleeping, eating, attending class, studying, working, gabbing, participating in sports, applying make-up, dating, etc. Then spend two to three times a day recording your activities and how much time you spend in each of these activities. This simple exercise will give you interesting information about yourself that can be of great value to you.

Next, setup an organizational structure by deciding how to use the time you have to your advantage. The old rule of spending two hours of study for every hour of class time is nice, but as you have probably noticed, it is seldom achievable or even practical. Besides, every class is unique, and the time you spend studying for each one will vary. The time you spend on each subject will also vary with the schools you attend. Some schools will have a sadistic teacher in English, some in history, sociology, or physiology.

The best approach to budgeting your time for each class involves three steps. First, estimate how much time is required to attend and study for each class. Of course, this will depend on your goals for that class, i.e., knowledge, interest, or grade. Make a schedule that allows ample time for each class. Do not be fooled and neglect the lesser unit classes. I remember my first semester of medical school when gross anatomy was the major hurdle. I was so taken up with this anatomy class that I neglected a seemingly lesser course in histology. I did great in anatomy, but that was at the price I paid for a mediocre grade in histology.

Second, it's important to be realistic when devising a study schedule. If you are accustomed to spending twenty hours a week studying, setting up a thirty-five hour a week schedule is only inviting disaster. The best way to break old habits and patterns is to give yourself positive, reinforcing experiences. If you lock yourself into an impossible schedule, you will be quickly frustrated and give up the idea altogether. If, however, your schedule is reasonable, then you will find that you can adhere to it, and your self-esteem will be boosted. That alone will often motivate you to study better and learn more.

Finally, be flexible when making up your schedule. Realize that the first schedule you set up is only a rough estimate of your time, and that it will need to be revised. Revisions should take place at least every two weeks. This will depend on the difficulty of certain sections in subjects, the dates that term papers are due, and the dates of quizzes and midterms. Do not be wed to the time blocks in your schedule, but for you own good, marry the idea of scheduling your time until graduation do you part.

A time schedule is a lot like a budget. If you are unreasonable or too rigid with the budget you set up, you will be quickly frustrated by the whole process and toss it to the wind. You will then feel worse than when you started for failing to follow through with something you began. If you are reasonable and flexible in setting it up, then the budget can be of enormous value and security to you, giving you helpful guidelines for spending your money—or in this case, your time—wisely.

The Plan of Attack

Have a systematic approach, or plan of attack, for each class you take. One of the best resources for this task is your class instructor. Students often think that teachers are too busy for them or that they do not want to be bothered with questions outside of class. Nothing could be further from the truth. Sure, there are those self-aggrandizing people who think their own projects are more important than their students, but they are usually the exception. It has been my experience that although most teachers are busy, they welcome personal contact with students and get tremendous satisfaction from showing students how to learn their discipline. Your teacher will likely be impressed by your interest in their class, and that may be an important point if your grade teeters on the borderline between A-B or B-C.

So approach the professor and take advantage of his or her experience and advice on how you should organize yourself for the class. After all, if instructors have spent six to eight years getting a master's degree or Ph.D. in a particular subject and have been teaching it for several years, they should be qualified to guide you through their forest. Of course, this isn't always the case, but it is, at least, a place to start.

Continuing this thought, it is worth your time to read the syllabus before you actually start the class. This serves two purposes. First, the syllabus is usually the instructor's way of introducing you to what lies ahead for you in the course and what is expected from you. Second, it gives you time to find another class if that one was not what you had in mind.

Many students never read the syllabus at any time during a course and only a few read it before the course begins. Be smart and get the big picture (which is often the syllabus) at the beginning of each semester.

Next, try to get together with people who have previously taken the class from the same teacher. This is a very valuable source of information. Find out from them:

1. How they approached the class;

2. What was expected from them in class

3. If there were any pop quizzes

4. What kind of exams were given and how they were graded

5. If they have copies of old exams (If the teacher does not object, get these at all costs.)

6. What is the best ways to approach specific instructors

7. What books were most useful for the class

It is obvious that if you have a choice, you should talk to someone who excelled in the class, but even an average student will be able to give you useful information. If you do not have access to someone who has had the same instructor for a class, it is still helpful to talk to someone who has taken the same class from another professor. He or she will also have valuable information to share. Do not neglect this gold mine of knowledge.

After you have read the syllabus and approached your professors and the students that have preceded you, check on the textbooks, the next important source of information for organizing your courses. As I mentioned above, ask other students what books are valuable for the class and what books have value only for starting bonfires. Some professors do not have the big picture or your checkbook in mind when they choose textbooks. There may be several more valuable sources available to you—so look for them. This is a very important point, and I will emphasize it at length in the next chapter.

Textbooks are written by experts in their fields, so the preface, introduction, and introductory chapters will give you important information on how to approach your subject and their book in particular. The first few chapters of the book almost always lay important foundations that are necessary to support the information in the rest of the book. See how the pros do it—read the introduction of your texts.

Note Organization

Organizing your notes efficiently can truly have lasting value. I will explore this topic further in Chapter six. If you do not organize and file your notes, papers, and exams after you have finished with them, they are almost certainly lost to you. What would you do if, at the end of a long year, while you were getting ready to head home for summer vacation, you looked at an eight-foot stack of old schoolwork piled in the corner?? Spend hours reliving the nightmare of each class, separating, organizing, and filing the papers individually? Probably not. If you're like most of us, you would say, "What the heck! I have the textbooks," then toss the papers into the trash, get in your car, and drive off. If you want to preserve this valuable source of information, buy yourself a filing cabinet, make one from orange crates or whatever, and use it. Believe me, I have gone back to my old notes and papers many times! You may spend up to thirty minutes a week labeling and filing your material, but it is time well spent and you will have something of lasting value for your academic and professional life.

Organize Yourself

Finally, organize yourself. I touched on discipline early in this chapter. I firmly believe that a disciplined and organized mind has the tools to accomplishing the goals you set. Discipline is the key to organization. Dr. Peck says that developing self-discipline involves learning four basic techniques:

How to delay gratification, which is a process of scheduling the pain and pleasure of life in such a way as to enhance the pleasure by meeting and experiencing the pain first and getting it over with. It is the only decent way to live. So save the frosting on the cake for last.

How to assume responsibility, which is realizing that you are in charge of you life and your education. You have the responsibility for the outcome, not some whim or chance, nor abundance of poor teachers, nor poor boyfriend or girlfriend selection. The outcome is up to you.

How to be dedicated to truth and reality. The truth is that you have sufficient resources, and the reality is that it takes hard work and often-long hours to prepare yourself to meet your goals.

The art of balancing, which Peck says is required to discipline, and is certainly needed if you want to develop wholeness in your life.

"The Big Picture" Organization

1. Discipline and organization are the basic tools required to solve life's problems

2. Organize your study time by first taking inventory of your available time.

3. Set up a realistic and flexible study schedule by estimating how much study time you need for each class and revising the schedule as your needs change.

4. Establish a systematic approach to each class by consulting with your teachers and with students who have taken the class previously.

5. Use the syllabus and study aids in your textbooks

6. Organize your notes to get lasting value from them.

7. Organize yourself by learning to delay gratification, to assume responsibility, to be dedicated to truth and reality, and to keep balance in your life.

CHAPTER FIVE

METHODS TO SANITY VERSUS MADDENING METHODS:

METHODS OF STUDY

STUDY METHODS CAN EITHER WORK TO YOUR advantage, or they can work toward your destruction. If your approach to thinking and studying is consistent and leads to assimilating material and coming to rational conclusions, then you have a beneficial method. If, however, your methods of thinking and studying are either haphazard or too rigid, you may find yourself in a very sick state of mind.

A former patient of mine used methods of thinking which were indeed maddening. She had a different method for controlling all the aberrant thoughts that came into her mind. She tried repeating the thoughts to herself in a different word sequence, moving her lips in a certain way to counteract the thoughts, and washing her hands compulsively to cleanse herself from the invading thoughts. Before she sought help, she reached the state of sitting isolated by

herself at home with the phone off the hook and the window shades drawn, spending all of their time trying to catch these thoughts as they came into her mind. She was letting her thoughts, and her methods for controlling them, rule her life. You see, your methods for studying can either be productive and economical, or as is usually the case, they can be frustrating and inefficient.

Everyone has different methods for studying. The clue is to develop an effective, systematic approach to learning that works for you. This is what this chapter is all about. In it I will examine an overall game plan for studying, the other necessary materials needed, preludes to methods, methods and how to get the big picture.

To start off, it is critical to do well in the beginning of the semester. This is essential to success in school and sets up to win. As many students discover, blowing off this part of the year is dangerous. It leaves you behind in classes, and you often miss important foundational material.

If you follow the principle of doing well in the beginning, it will have at least three positive effects on you and your semester. First, your effort will be on establishing a solid foundation, and as we have seen before, building knowledge on a good foundation is a lot easier than building on one made of sand.

Second, by working hard during the first part of the semester, you will do well in the class and subsequently build your self-esteem. With your confidence intact, it will be easier for you to continue in a positive and productive way. You will feel good about yourself because your efforts will have paid off. This is a lot easier to do in the beginning because the material is usually more introductory and therefore easier to grasp and build on than later in the semester. If you miss that foundation, even your greatest efforts will not take you as far as they could have and you will have less incentive to keep up a good effort.

Third, if you do well in the beginning, then you will leave yourself some breathing room in the event that something unexpected comes up and you miss some study time. Also, you will do better in your classes, because you will be under less pressure to perform, and people learn best when they are free from drastic time constraints.

This foundational principle is one of the chief reasons for my success in college and medical school. By obtaining a solid foundation, developing self-confidence, being rewarded for my effort, and leaving myself breathing room to learn under less pressure, I was able to achieve my immediate academic goals.

The other aspect of this game plan involves learning how *not* to spend the semester going from test to test. This is a common syndrome in college and is almost the norm in medical school. Many students survive in school only by studying for only one test at a time—the one three days from now—leaving all other work until after the exam. But as my own psychiatric work with students will verify, there is a price to pay for this method of madness in the form of ulcers, high blood pressure, and insomnia. Learn how to schedule your time not just during a particular study session, but throughout the semester (refer to Chapter four). If you adhere to a reasonable schedule, you can eliminate or at least decrease the test-to-test study syndrome. This will give you a healthier outlook, mind, and body, and will give me less work to do as a psychiatrist.

Necessary Other Materials

Many students believe that their education begins and ends with the first and last pages of their textbooks. They do not realize that there are many "other" materials that can be even more valuable to them than their text. Specifically, I am referring to three sources: review books, recent magazine articles, and old exams.

Review books. I call these "big picture" books. These give you the straight stuff that you need to remember. These resources are great to get a quick overview and are very useful for review. Do not, however, use them as your only source. If you do, usually the facts will not make as much sense as they should. Find out about these books from your teaches or fellow students, or by going to the library or book store. Start using these sources as much as possible. They will save you a lot of time and improve your study methods if used properly.

Recent magazine articles. If you train yourself in school to be informed on the latest developments in your field of interest, you will carry this trait with you into your professional life. Periodical literature, besides giving you the most current information, often will present a topic more clearly and concisely than your textbook. Find the magazines that are most beneficial to your studies and then use the information in them to your advantage.

Old exams. Get these if your professor or your conscience does not mind! Old tests are as valuable a resource as your textbook, lecture notes, or review books. They illustrate how your instructor writes test questions and how to answer the questions. Studying old exams is also an excellent review method for testing yourself on the material. Finally, teachers have a difficult time making up new test questions each year, so you will find many questions on old tests essentially the same as the questions on the current test. Be smart and try to get copies of old tests from previous students or the instructor.

Preludes to Methods

Before I discuss the different methods of study, I am going to mention a few points that I call "preludes to methods." These are simple statements or principles that I believe are basic to good study methods.

Before beginning a study session, quickly review the material you studied the day before. This will increase your exposure to it and will also give you an opportunity to test your understanding and recall of it.

Study material in well-defined units. Before each study session, carefully and systematically choose a block of material to be covered. In this way you will have specific goals for you time and can regulate the amount of material that you cover. It is easier to master definite sections of material than ill-defined amounts of it.

If you are having trouble with a statement that is poorly written, try to rephrase it in your own words. This technique will also help you better retain what you learn.

Learning follows understanding. If you understand what you have memorized, then you have learned the material. On the other hand, if you know the facts cold but cannot make sense of them, you may ace the test, but still have wasted your time.

Apply what you learn. At every opportunity available, try to take what you have learned and find a practical application for it. Application is integral to retention.

If you are having problems in the beginning of a class, check your foundation. It is better to shape up your foundation early on than to waste a semester in confusion.

Methods

There are four specific study methods that I used in different combinations during my academic career: Preview/Summary, Test-Making, Underlining, and Outlining.

Preview/Summary. Getting an overview before you dive into a subject and then summarizing what you have learned are the two necessary principles for getting the big picture. If you practice reading the summaries and skimming the material as you begin, you know what to expect during your session, and you can develop a plan for completing your task. This increases your efficiency.

Also, as your study session is nearing its conclusion, take a few minutes to write a short summary of what you have learned. This practice reinforces your understanding and gives you insight into particular problem areas. So, the first method is preview and review. This tells you where you are going and where you have been—two thirds of the work.

Test-Making. One of my favorite study methods is to make up test questions during and after a study session. By doing this, you learn to pick out important facts and reinforce what you have studied. If you write these questions, you will have a good, quick source of review to consult right before an exam. When I studied, I kept a separate piece of paper with my own questions on one side and the answers on the back. Often I would have 30 to 50 percent of the real test figured out on those sheets of paper.

It is obvious that if you have questions on the material you are studying, you should also write these down and seek clarification from the instructor or other sources. Keeping a record of questions about material you do not understand is helpful in review, because if you had trouble with the material initially, you will likely need more review to master it.

Making up your own test questions as well as writing down questions about material you do not understand takes time and will slow you down initially. However, this practice will help you eliminate having to read through the textbook or your notes four to five times before you assimilate the material. Thus, it will save you time and energy in the long run.

Underlining. Underlining textbooks or notes is a very popular method of study, and if used properly, it can be a valuable tool in your study arsenal. However, this method is often overdone. There was a student in my medical school class who would drive the sanest man to madness with his psychedelic underlining methods. He used fourteen different colors, underlining virtually everything in his text or notes, using different colors to denote the degree of importance for the material. If you looked at his material after he was through underlining, you would have the kaleidoscopic feelings that are often reported during LSD trips.

Underlining the material you are studying is effective for three reasons. First, it helps you focus on the important material. Obviously, if you underline everything, you are wasting your time. Select the summary sentence of a paragraph, the fact statements, and important supporting material. Underline what you want to remember, and what you think might be on the exam.

Second, underlining helps you to be active in your learning. Selecting important statements to underline forces you to take an active role in studying so that you will be less likely to passively read through the material. You will interact with it, instead.

Third, underlining helps you to review. If you have the pertinent points highlighted, then you can quickly review what you have studied. If you have underlined everything, you will have to plod through all of it to review, a time-waster at a point when you usually don't have much time.

Outlining. Outlining what you are studying is the most time-consuming method of all. It has advantages and disadvantages. If it is done concisely and thoughtfully, its positive points are as follows.

First, you re-expose yourself to the material in a slower and more methodical manner, thus increasing the chance for greater retention.

Second, you again take an active role in your studies by deciding what information is important enough to rewrite. It is easy to underline everything in a book, but when you outline, you will force yourself to restate only the important material (unless you have masochistic tendencies).

Third, you will have a valuable tool for review, saving yourself hours when it is time to study for the test. Many students, even after they have underlined their texts, never go back to their books before the exam. They rely on their notes and crib sheets. If you have another set of notes that can be reviewed quickly, you will be more likely to use them.

There are two major disadvantages to outlining:

First, this method is very time-consuming, and if you are very busy, you will have trouble doing it consistently.

Second, this method is only for the patient individual who can see the value of slowly going through new material. If you are the type who wants to study as quickly as possible, you should not cultivate your outlining skills. If you decide to outline, you should highlight the important facts of new material in a consistent fashion. Be concise and be prepared to have a thorough set of notes.

In conclusion, realize that you are unique. After you have given each study method a fair trial, choose the methods that work best for you. Remember, using a good study method every day will help keep the madness away!

"The Big Picture" Methods to Sanity vs. Maddening Methods

1. Do your best in the first part of the semester. This will help you establish a solid foundation, build your self-esteem, and leave you some breathing room.

2. Use the "other" materials: review books, magazine articles, and old exams to your advantage. There is more to education than textbooks.

3. Begin study sessions with a quick review of previous work; study well-defined units; reword poorly written statements; learn by first understanding and then applying what you learn.

4. Use overview and summary techniques.

5. Create test questions for yourself to check your comprehension and learn how to choose important facts.

6. Use underlining to focus, be active, and review.

7. Outline only if you are a patient person; it is thorough but time consuming.

CHAPTER SIX

IT'S A CLASS ACT:

CLASS SKILLS

A SCREAMING FIVE-YEAR OLD CLUTCHES HIS mommy's leg and looks as though Godzilla's uncle is waiting for him behind the classroom door. Then he pleads with his mommy, "Why do I have to go to kindergarten?" Years later, that same student' social skills have improved, and he has given up the idea of screaming and leg-clutching. Yet he still asks the same question over and over: "Why do I have to go to class?" Rationalization skills have also improved. He leaves Godzilla's relatives out of the argument and contends that he can get the necessary information from expensive text-books, or that the classes are so boring that someone could get rich by taping and selling the lectures to incurable insomniacs.

If you are unskilled in the art of using class time, then the above rationalizations are reasonable and going to class may be largely wasted time for you. If, however, you become artful at the skills needed to operate at peak efficiency during class, your time in lectures will be very profitable and help you greatly reduce your study time.

Why Should I Go to Class?

Before I discuss the specific skills necessary for making lectures a successful experience, I first want to answer the question, "Why should I go to class?" There are many reasons for attending class. You can have the teacher clarify questionable points for you. You can meet other students and see how they approach the class. Hopefully, you will be able to find a compatible study partner. Of course, if attendance is required, you can make sure that you are not dropped from the roster.

I feel that the most important reason for going to class is the lecture itself. During the lecture, you will usually be taught several important things besides the material itself: how to learn the subject; what information the instructor thinks is important; what will be on exams (important clues for exams are almost always given in class); and how to assimilate the subject so that it will have practical value for you. If you master the lecture, your study time will decrease significantly because you will know what is important and how to go about learning and assimilating it. Don't cheat yourself. Go to class and get the most out of lectures.

Be Prepared

Once you have decided to attend class faithfully, the next important step is to prepare yourself for what is going to happen there. As I said earlier, preparation is paramount to accomplishment. Accomplish all you can in class by being prepared.

The first thing you need to prepare for class is yourself. This means you need to get enough sleep the night before. You should also eat very little before class so you will be able to stay awake. Eating a big meal before a class will make you tired as your body works to digest all that food. Also, being in good physical shape will make it easier for you to concentrate.

In preparing for a class, read the section of the syllabus that deals with the upcoming lecture to find out what is going to be happening in class that day. Believe me, it is very disheartening to get to class and discover that the midterm is scheduled, or that your term paper is due. Read the course outline and find out what is happening and when.

Next, if possible, read the section of the text that deals with upcoming class. This serves three purposes. First, it familiarizes you with new vocabulary words, thus decreasing the distraction of asking your friend, "What's a cluster headache? Could it be this class?" While your friend laughs at your question, you both have missed the next three important points. Second, reading ahead gives you the opportunity to solidify new information, because the lecture will be your second exposure to the material. After reading the text you may have some unanswered questions, which you can then ask in class. Third, you will be able to intelligently participate in class, which will further solidify the material as well as impress the instructor (which is not the goal, but certainly cannot hurt, if you need the grade).

Goal Setting

After you have prepared yourself, read the course outline for the upcoming class, and have tried to read the material ahead of time, set specific goals for each class. These goals may include getting the instructor to answer your questions, seeing what the instructor emphasizes in a certain section, and trying to figure out what he or she will ask on the exam.

One goal that I always had when preparing for class was to try to get a copy of the teacher's lecture notes. This was not always possible, because many teachers lecture from memory or do not want their notes copied. It has been my experience, however, that most teachers have extensive notes on their lecture topic. If they are approached in the right way, they are happy to let students copy them. The advantages of having these notes are obvious: You will not have to get writer's cramp from taking notes because you can follow along as the lecture is presented; you will not have to worry that your notes are incomplete; and you will often find the important points underlined or starred, emphasizing what the teacher thinks is important. Your teacher's notes are very valuable tools. It doesn't hurt to ask—so ask for them!

A Short Word

A word about notebook organization is warranted here. I have found that loose-leaf paper in a three-ring binder gave me the most flexibility and was the easiest to organize. There are also several computer programs and PDA (personal digital assistants) that are on the market that also help with organization.

Staying Awake

One of my high school professors had a sure way of keeping students awake in his ninth grade religion class. He was a Carmelite Brother at a Catholic high school in California. He was also a former heavyweight boxer who stood six feet four inches tall and weighed about 230 pounds. The incident occurred early in the semester when one of his students fell asleep with his head in his arms. It was after lunch and he had eaten too much. The brother continued his lecture as he walked to this napping student and stood behind him with a glint of his glory days in his eyes. After about ten seconds of staring at him, the brother landed his large, swift fist in a direct blow, striking an area that would be a painful reminder that you do not fall asleep in God's class. From then on the students in his class carried toothpicks with them to keep their eyelids open in case they started to get heavy—which they never did again!

If you find that you are falling asleep in class and you do not have a Carmelite Brother to help you break the habit, then here are a few suggestions that may help. First, try light exercise before class. Taking a walk with a friend or doing limbering exercises increases your heart rate and helps you feel more alert. If this does not have any effect on your narcolepsy (brief attacks of deep sleep during the day), then I suggest you try to participate as much as possible in class. If you keep your mind busy, you will be less likely drop off.

Another helpful technique for keeping the sandman away during class is to sit as near to the front of the room as possible. It is embarrassing to fall asleep in class, and if you are in direct view of the lecturer, then you will be less likely to snooze. Sitting near the front is useful even if you do not have narcoleptic tendencies. It helps you see the teacher better, enabling you to pick up nonverbal cues that would not be as evident from farther away. Sitting close to the front also lessens distractions, because it is not as easy to gab, write notes, or flirt close to the front.

Hearing Does Not Equal Listening

As I begin the section of this chapter on listening skills in class, many of you may be asking, "Why do I need to read about how to listen? I've been doing it all of my life." Just because you have been doing something for a long time does not necessarily mean you are doing it well. Many medical students have been writing for more than twenty years, but to see their chicken scratching, you would think they were about to begin their first class in remedial penmanship. Besides, if you take a poll among parents and children, husbands and wives, you will invariably find that their significant others lack at least some measure of skill in listening.

There are five important steps for effective listening in classroom situations. First, you need to be in a position to adequately hear the lecturer. Do this by sitting close to the front, keeping distractions out of sight, and by asking the professor to speak up if you are having trouble hearing him or her.

Next, you need to process what you hear. Hearing, by itself, gives you little or no information, you hear many things every day that you never process, i.e., street noise, birds chirping, a child asking a parent the same question for the twentieth time, and many radio and TV programs. You need to take an active part in processing what you hear in order to understand what is being said.

Third, you need to acknowledge that you have heard and processed the information. A classroom situation is a two-way street and must involve feedback to the professor as the material is being presented. Otherwise, you could just listen to lecture tapes. If the professor does not think that anyone is paying attention to the lecture, his enthusiasm will diminish as well as his ability to teach an interesting and stimulating class, although that may be the reason no one is listening in the first place! We all need feedback, so acknowledge the lecturer with nods when you understand what is being said or with questions when you do not. This is part of being an active listener.

The fourth step involves how you react to the lecture. If you are hearing, processing, and acknowledging what is being presented during the lecture, you will usually (unless writing takes all of your time) react to it on an emotional level. This can be good, or it can be harmful. It can be good if you agree with what is being said, because you will then feel an emotional bond with the professor. It can also be good if you disagree with what is being presented, because you can dialogue on the subject, thus increasing your knowledge and maybe even increasing the instructor's. Reacting emotionally to material presented in class can be harmful if you disagree with the teacher and subsequently write him or her off as uninformed or incompetent. Disagreement is valuable for examining and solidifying your own stand on a subject. People who do not think like you still have much to offer, maybe more than someone you agree with. Be tolerant and get as much information from your instructor as you can.

Assimilation is the final task of a good listener. This occurs after you have heard, processed, acknowledged, and reacted to what was presented in class. It involves making the information part of yourself. You can accomplish this step only if you have the big picture of the lecture in mind and understand how and why the information is important for the class and your educational goals. If you can take what was said and give practical meaning to it, assimilation is taking place. If you are near the end of a lecture and are having trouble doing this, ask the instructor to put it together for you. Do not be the first three letters of assimilation! Discover the importance of what you are doing and how it all fits into the big picture before you leave each class. It will make you an active listener, with knowledge, understanding, *and* grades to show for it.

Taking Notes

Balancing the skills of listening and note taking in class is not an easy task. It is very difficult to hear, process, acknowledge, react, and assimilate anything if you are constantly finding yourself three major points behind the lecture.

In order to be a good listener in class, you need to be a swift and efficient note-taker. If you are an efficient typist you can also take notes on a laptop if it is allowed. It is also helpful to have a copy of the teacher's lecture notes or a very good handout in front of you during the lecture. Since this is not always possible, however, and learn to take good notes.

Most of the reasons for taking good notes are obvious. They are a way of having an accurate record of what was said in class. You may think that you have a very good memory, but each semester the average student spends more than 250 hours in lectures. Those first few weeks of class will seem decades away when it's time for finals.

Notes are also the best source for reviewing for exams. My experience has been that more than 75 percent of the test material for most courses is covered in the lectures. If your notes are good and you know them, that is usually an automatic 75 percent or more on a test. The rest is icing on the cake. If you have a good set of notes, you will decrease study time because you will have most of the important material in front of you, and you will have more direction about how to learn it.

Another reason for taking good notes is that you will then have them when you need to study for you finals and any national exams that you might take, i.e., SAT, GRE, MCAT, LSAT, etc. Also, as I learned over and over again, notes can be a valuable reference source in years to come.

What steps are necessary for becoming an efficient note-taker? First, your notes need to be readable. If you cannot make sense of your notes, there is no sense in spending the time taking them. Write as clearly as you can. If your scrawl looks as though it has been through the washer, then print.

Next, label your notes with the date, teacher's name, and the specific subject of the lecture. This will help you organize them when studying for exams and will also help you to file them. Use abbreviations to speed up your note taking. It does not matter if you make them up, just be consistent in their usage. Some common ones that I use are:

W/	with
W/O	without
W/I	within
&	and
e.g.	for example
i.e.	that is
@	at
X	times
Etc.	et cetera

If you have trouble making up your own abbreviations for common words you use a lot, consult a good dictionary, which should have an extensive list of abbreviations.

If you are still having trouble keeping up with the lecturer, ask him or her to slow down. Most will be glad to do so and welcome the feedback. Chances are if you are having trouble keeping up, so are many other students. Another option is to bring a tape recorder to class, if allowed, and take notes on the lecture later.

Next, organize your lecture notes. Teachers usually follow an outline when they lecture. If you can incorporate this outline into your notes, the notes will be easier to follow and refer to later. If you cannot detect an outline in the lecture, then roughly make your own as you go along. Use subheadings to title the material as you go along.

When taking notes, be sure that you leave yourself plenty of room to fill in gaps that will inevitably occur. Also, it is a good idea to leave a wide margin at the left hand side of the paper. This will enable you to put main ideas in the margin to indicate what is in the body of the notes. Do not write so small that you will need an electron microscope to decipher your notes. One classmate of mine could fit more works on a sheet of paper than a reducing copier. The eyestrain from trying to decipher too-small writing can cause headaches and make you very irritable.

It is very helpful to have another, trusted person in your class with whom you can compare notes. This practice will help both of you to fill in the gaps and check your accuracy.

How much should you write? I have known students who sit back and try, by osmosis, to assimilate the material just by hearing the lecture. I have also known students who compulsively write down every word that is said. It is obvious that the answer lies somewhere in between these two extremes. If you are having trouble striking a balance, make sure that you tip the scale toward the compulsive note-taker's side. Copious notes are worthwhile; you can eliminate the excess when you have time to go through your notes later.

The most important clues on how much to write will come from the instructor. The more effort it takes him or her to explain the material to you, the more you should take notice of what he or she is trying to say. Again, the syllabus takes a great deal of effort to prepare, so know what is in it. If a teacher writes something on the board, write it in your notes. It takes effort to do that, so appreciate the effort and whatever point the teacher is trying to emphasize.

Next, watch for verbal and nonverbal cues in the lecture. If a teacher says that something is important, why doubt it? After all, this is usually the person who is going to make up the test. If the teacher explains something three different ways, take note and be sure you have the point on paper. If a teacher pauses and looks as if he or she is waiting for you to write down the point, write it down. Watch for changes in voice tone and listen to the emphasis that is placed on words. Also be aware of what the teacher's body language is telling you. Learn to observe and really get to know your instructors. It is a skill to be able to read them, and the only way to become skillful at this is to make a conscious effort to try to put what they say and how they say it together.

If, when taking notes, it becomes obvious that you do not understand a specific point, put a big question mark next to it so that you can refer back to it and have it clarified. Likewise, if you know that something is important, underline or star it so that you remember its importance later. And by all means, if a professor says that something is going to be on a test, believe him or her and make an appropriate notation of the fact.

Make sure that you first have the big picture of what is being said. Then fill in as many details as you and the teacher deem necessary. Remember, take your cues from the lecturer.

The last point I want to make on note taking involves persevering to the end. The last ten to fifteen minutes of a class are usually very important. The teacher usually summarizes the main points and often illustrates their practical usage. He or she will also tell you what to expect next time. Many students are so impatient for the class to end (constantly looking at their watches or the classroom clock, hoping that the lecturer will see them and get the hint) that they miss some important information. Be attentive to the end. After all, you or your parents are paying the bill—get your money's worth.

Also remember that assigning textbook chapters takes the least amount of the teacher's effort. Reading the text should take place in conjunction with note taking in class. This is a very important point! You will do well if you are already familiar with the material to be presented in class.

Questions

Asking the right questions is the most important step to getting the right answer. It is a sign of curiosity and indicates a willingness to learn. The fear of appearing stupid, however, often prevents questions and stifles the learning process. This fear, for those who hold themselves back, outweighs the fear of ignorance, which should be a much more frightening prospect.

How many times have you wanted to ask a question, yet, when it came to saying the words, fear or embarrassment kept your mouth shut? How many times have you not gotten the information you needed from the teacher because of the fear that you would be a nuisance to him or her? You may be the victim of misconceptions.

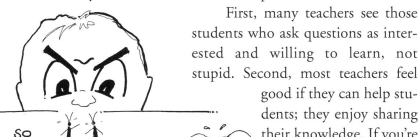

First, many teachers see those students who ask questions as interested and willing to learn, not stupid. Second, most teachers feel good if they can help students; they enjoy sharing their knowledge. If you're bothering them, you will probably be able to tell, and you can ask them another time. Even better, you can start by asking if this is a good time for them to answer a question.

In any class, if you are reasonably prepared but you begin to feel lost in the material, most likely other students share your feeling and appreciate your questions. I have found that most professors also appreciate questions, because it indicates that students are paying attention and helps the professors do a better job of teaching you.

Likewise, in business, if you do not have all the information you need to do your job, but you are afraid to appear stupid by asking questions, think of how much worse you'll feel when it's discovered you're not doing the job right. Most supervisors want to teach because they, like most of us, get satisfaction from helping others to do something well, especially if they're held responsible for the kind of job you do.

There is no doubt that the failure to ask questions and gather information damages many relationships. When we are confused about others' behavior or think we may have gotten the wrong information from them, it is crucial to clarify the meaning of their behavior. Without clarification, our assumptions take over, and harmless misunderstandings turn into menacing monsters.

The worst thing that can happen when you ask a question in class is that the teacher may refuse to answer it, give you an answer you don't like, or make you feel stupid for asking. I think ignorance is worse than those three things combined. You can lessen the chances of a negative response by asking questions in an appropriately respectful way at the right time. But when you have questions, ASK THEM! They will get you more information, which will bring you closer to your goals.

Not knowing how or where to get information also holds many students back from their desires. The best remedy for this, however, is to ask the right questions of the right people. When that is not possible, there are other ways to gather information. Internet search engines are the most common place to get information quickly. Public school and university libraries have information on almost anything. They have trained staffs of information gatherers. Yet many people do not know how to use libraries. If you are one of them, learn. Where do you learn? Ask a librarian. The library is a great information source, and you can't beat the cost.

Expecting yourself to know something without being taught is what psychiatrists call magical thinking. It is like a person who has never been somewhere before refusing to ask for directions when he is lost. This magical thinking of "I should know the answers" afflicts many students. You are in school to learn. You are not born with the answers. Don't expect yourself to know answers before you have been taught the material. Be good at asking for help. Pride is often an excuse to cover ignorance. Be kind to yourself and don't expect more from yourself than is reasonable. If you don't know something, admit it, then find the answer to it.

Here are some other suggestions about asking good questions. Make them pertinent. It's said that there is no such thing as a stupid question. If you had attended class with me and heard a particular student ask the sort of questions that even trivia books would consider trivial, you would agree that some questions are indeed stupid and inappropriate. Be sensitive and do not waste your classmates' valuable time. Only ask questions that relate specifically to the subject matter.

Be as specific in your questioning as possible. If you leave the question open-ended, the teacher might go off on a tangent have trouble finishing the lecture, and so hurry to finish, possibly leaving out information he or she intended to cover.

Asking questions about areas where you disagree with the teacher is perfectly acceptable as long as you do it in a respectful manner. If you do not agree with a professor and want him to further defend his position on a subject, that's OK, too. It is one of the best ways for students and teachers to learn. If the teacher is truly knowledgeable on the subject, he or she will not be threatened by you. Learning to dialogue about disagreements is good skill to acquire in life.

Finally, when you ask questions in class, be aware of other students. Do not hog class time with your questions; give others a chance to question and dialogue. Also, if you have a question near the end of the class, try to save the question until after class. Being polite is another good skill to acquire.

Asking Questions after Class

After class is over, what then? First, go to the professor and clarify any questions you had in your notes. The sooner you clear up these questions, the better.

Next, recopy your notes as soon after class as possible. This serves several important functions. First, it allows you to reorganize them and to make them more readable. This practice will give you a more ordered set of notes.

Second, rewriting your notes gives you the opportunity to fill in the gaps of your notes and answer any questions you had about them during class time. A complete set of notes will serve you well when test time draws near.

Third, when you recopy and complete your notes, you expose yourself to the material a second time. It is a well-known fact that if you review the material within a short time after class, you will remember it longer than if you do not see it again for two weeks.

Fourth, as you rewrite your notes, you can make up questions about important information that you think will be on the test. Write these in your new set of notes. If you practice, you can become so good at anticipating what will be on exams, that you can answer a majority of the test questions in your notes. See how good you are at getting on the teacher's wavelength.

Finally, recopying notes will give you a chance to make a companion set of "big picture" fact sheets. These notes contain only major points and are used for quick study immediately before an exam. If you write these sheets as you go, they will be of tremendous value to you. This is a way of making sure you get the big picture.

A good set of recopied notes will be beneficial to you for a long time. If you do not buy this idea, at least go over your notes within seventy-two hours for re-exposure and to fill in the gaps.

Now that I have shared my experience in the art of attending class, I am going to end this chapter by sharing with you one more tool that will serve you well in class. I have found this tool of tremendous value in helping me obtain dates during class. Here is a sample of my technique, and I might modestly add that it averaged a 92 percent positive response rate!

Dear Robbin:

I know that you do not know me except for this class, but I would really like to have the pleasure of your company at dinner with me this Friday. Please answer below by checking the appropriate box or boxes.

1. Yes
2. No
3. Maybe later.
4. You must be kidding me. Please say you are kidding!
5. You'd have better luck with your cadaver!
6. I don't like guys who write these stupid notes!
7. Love is blind, but I have put on my glasses.
8. I hope a herd of dragonflies beat you to death with their wings.

If yes, or another time, please place your phone number below:

_____

If no, please do not return this, since I am not good at handling rejection.

Daniel

Use what works!!!

"The Big Picture" It's a Class Act

1. Go to class to increase your knowledge, clarify questions, interact with other students, find a compatible study partner, and keep you attendance record in order.

2. Prepare for class by using mild exercise to increase alertness, sitting close to the front of the room, and realizing that what is said in class is usually on the exams.

3. Effective listening in class involves hearing, processing, acknowledging, reacting, and assimilating.

4. Lecture notes are usually your best review source for exams.

5. In note-taking use abbreviations, write as clearly as possible, ask the professor to slow down if you are having trouble keeping up, leave plenty of room for the main ideas on the margins, and compare your notes with another student.

6. In deciding how much to write, be aware of the teacher's effort to emphasize certain points and watch for verbal and nonverbal cues.

7. In asking questions, keep to the point, ask the questions as soon as they come up, be specific, and be polite.

8. Recopy your notes to improve their neatness, reorganize them, fill in the gaps, re-expose yourself to them, and make up your own test questions and "big picture" fact sheets.

CHAPTER SEVEN

PARIETAL RELATIONS:
MEMORIZE FASTER WITH BETTER RETENTION

ARGYLE MET THREE FENDERLESS VALIANTS, while Lucy tripped on his lice. I know this sounds like a great beginning of a science fiction novel where the main character, a sock, meets three cars in the bad section of Los Angeles after their fenders have been ripped off. Meanwhile, the sock's owner, a man named Lucy, is tripping over some very large lice. (Certainly stranger things have happened in California). This crazy picture survives many years after my friend, Alan Richardson, M.D., coined it to help us remember the ten essential amino acids (protein building blocks). This is one of the best examples of how to use the parietal lobe of your brain in memory.

Arg/ile (**arginine, isolucine**)

Met (**methionine**)

Three (**threonine**)

Fenderless (<u>phenyl</u>alanine)

V<u>ali</u>ants (valine) while

L<u>ucy</u> (<u>leuci</u>ne)

Tr<u>ipp</u>ed (tr<u>yp</u>tophan) on

H<u>is</u> (h<u>is</u>tadine)

Lic<u>e</u> (l<u>ys</u>ine)

This technique works because of the very powerful associative properties that exist in the parietal lobe of your brain. All Alan did was to take things that he knew— argyle socks, fenders, lice, etc.—and associate them with new material that he wanted to remember. He stored the information in his brain as he learned it. These associations then provided a place for him to start looking for the material when he needed to retrieve it.

Being able to recall what you have learned has infinite value for students. This skill can be enhanced by several memory techniques. To begin, let me give you a quick overview of the three types of memory processes that you possess: immediate, short-term, and long-term memory.

Immediate Memory

Your immediate memory enables you to remember information just long enough to apply it or to respond to it. You use your immediate memory when you take notes on a lecture and when you rewrite those notes, every time you transcribe a few words. As you read this book, you continually use it to give yourself the chance to process what is printed. Paying attention is the best way to increase your immediate memory capability. Your immediate memory processes the material coming in. You then decide whether to discard this material or to put it into your short-term memory bank.

Short-Term Memory

Your short-term memory allows you to temporarily store several pieces of information. The loss of this type of memory is one of the hallmarks of senility. In diagnosing this syndrome, I will ask the person to remember three things, for example: a 1966 Chevy, a red ball, and Lombard Street in San Francisco. Then I will ask the person to repeat it several minutes later. The senile patient, having an impaired short-term memory, will usually not respond correctly.

You can enhance your short-term memory by concentrating on the information to be retained, understanding the information in its context, and grouping similar pieces of information together. Short-term memory serves as a transition between immediate and long-term memory. After deciding to retain something, you remember it long enough in your short-term memory to work on its long-term retention. Then it is deposited into your long-term memory bank.

Long-Term Memory

Long-term memory involves the retention of material beyond a few minutes at at a time to days, weeks, and even years at a time. The number of items that can be stored in your long-term memory is limitless. Undoubtedly, you have subconsciously found many ways to organize and retrieve the information stored here. If you go one step further and systematically order the material you want to remember into tangible associations that your parietal lobe can catalog for you, you can easily store and retrieve more information at time.

These three types of memory operate interdependently. In order to deposit information into your long-term memory bank, you must first make substantial deposits into your immediate and short-term memory accounts.

Why Memory Fails

Before I outline the specific techniques for improving your long-term memory, I will discuss four common reasons why memory fails. First, there is an initial lack of focus on important details. If you do not pay attention to what is being presented, the material will not enter any of your three memory systems. It will be lost before there is any chance of assimilation. This is often the reason why we have a hard time remembering names—we do not focus on them when we first hear them. This is why it is so important to avoid distractions during class lectures; you need to focus on the material being presented so that you can begin processing it.

The second common reason your memory fails is because you do not understand the material you are trying to absorb or memorize. Absent-mindedly repeating phrases that you do not understand is a poor way to study and is an inefficient use of your time.

Third, your memory will fail if you do not get the big picture. If you cannot place the details of the material to be retained into a larger context, the information will be scattered throughout your brain like fallen leaves blown about in autumn. Get the big picture first; it will help your understanding and therefore your memory.

Finally, a lack of motivation will result in a lack of memory. If you do not see the point of memorizing something, you will have a hard time putting forth the effort to do it. If you need to convince yourself of its importance, then do it promptly. Your time is valuable. I know this may involve some fancy selling to yourself, but it is for a good cause.

Turning these points around, the first four things that you can do to improve your memory are:

1. Pay attention and focus on what is being presented
2. Realize understanding comes before retention
3. Remember that it is easier to put details into a big picture than into a scattered brain
4. See the need to understand and memorize the material

Tools for Building a Better Memory

Many educators say that memory aids have no place in education, that if you understand something, you will remember it. Neither of these ideas are helpful. Memory aids are extremely valuable for helping you retain concepts and their supporting facts. They can save you time and increase your retention dramatically.

There are six tools that I have used successfully in school to improve my ability to store and retain material. All of these methods involve using associations between information already possessed and the information that needs to be stored. These techniques will help you become an active learner, and any time that you combine activity with study, your chances of retention are greater.

The first of these mnemonics (anything that assists your memory) is a very helpful tool that Loisette* wrote about in 1899. The technique provides a simple code for translating numbers into certain letters. This makes it easy to remember any series of numbers by just making up the appropriate words or sentences, using the letters that correspond with the numbers. An example of this system is:

Number	Consonants	Rationale
1	t, d	t has one down stroke, d is a 0+1 = 1
2	n	n has two down strokes
3	m	m has three down strokes
4	r	r is the fourth letter of "four"
5	l	capital L is the Roman numeral for 50
6	g, j	script is an upside-down six, and capital J looks like a backward 6
7	k, hard c	k can be combined with 7, hard c sounds like k
8	f	both 8 and script f have 2 loops
9	p, b	backward p or upside-down b is nine

| 0 | z, s | z is the first letter of zero and s looks like a backward z |

*In this system all other consonants and vowels have no number value.

You can master this code in ten minutes or less, and it will be one of the most profitable 600 seconds of your life! You see, you can then translate any number into a word, or sequence of words that can be easily associated in your brain. For instance, if you need to remember the date that Thomas Jefferson first took office as our third president in 1801, then that is easy if you recall Thomas faced a sever test, or T(1) F(8) S(0) T(1), as presidents often do. If you want to remember that your sweetheart's birthday is September 21, think of pant (9-21); the connection should be obvious. And, if you need to remember an important appointment on March 31 at 8:10, recall: Meet me at office at sundown (3-31, 8:10). You can use your keys as the first letter of a series of words, or as all of the keyed letters in a word. Its use in remembering dates, times and any other number is limited only by your imagination.

Second, rhymes are a very popular tool for recalling rules or organization:

"I before E except after C;"

"Spring forward in Spring, fall back in Fall;"

"Thirty days hath September, April, June and November."

Rhymes help connect items, that otherwise seem totally unrelated, into a metrical pattern. They are very good at establishing definite orders, because any mistake in the order of recall will destroy the rhyme.

The following rhyme aids in retaining a sequence of facts:

> One is a bun.
> Two is a shoe,
> Three is a tree,
> Four is a door,
> Five is a hive,
> Six are stick,
> Seven is heaven
> Eight is a gate,
> Nine is a line, and
> Ten is a hen.

Choose ten facts that you need to remember in a precise order and mentally picture an association between each of them and their corresponding number's object. In less than a few minutes you can easily memorize their order. Try this method with unrelated facts to observe its usefulness to you.

Third, use places to remember specific things. The Greek poet Simonides was said to have left a banquet just before the roof collapsed and killed all those inside. Even though many bodies were not identifiable, Simonides was able to identify them by their place at the table.

The practical use of this technique involves placing an associative object into a certain location. Then by going back in your mind to the location, the object or fact should come back to you. For example, in memorizing a speech that is organized and outlined, choose the ideas or the major subdivisions and associate them in some way with the different rooms in you home. As you are delivering the speech, imagine yourself walking from room to room discovering the associations you have made in the proper order. If you practice this technique, your associative powers will be come limited only by the number of locations you can think of.

Fourth, the use of acronystic words or phrases (formed from the initial letters of words) can be very helpful. When I have a series of facts to memorize, the first thing I do is to tally their first letters to see if I can arrange them into an associative word or phrase. A few examples of this method include: "On old Olympus' towering top, a Finn and German viewed a hop." Each first letter corresponds to the first letter of the twelve cranial nerves in their proper order: Olfactory, optic, ocular, trochlear, trigeminal, abduceus, facial, acoustic, glossal pharyngeal, vagus, accessory and hypoglossal.

SHIT acronyzes the major causes for hematuria (blood in the urine): kidney stones, hematologic (blood) problems, infections, tumors, trauma, and tuberculosis. You may object to this word, but if you notice blood in your urine, then it might be one of the first things you say, thus the association!

BRASS is used by marksmen to remember the steps in firing a rifle: breathe, relax, aim, stabilize and squeeze.

The more colorful the acronym, the greater the chance that it will be easily remembered. During the last eight years I have compiled well over five hundred of these, and even though I do not recall all of them, I remembered them for the exam or for as long as I need them. Practice this method – your memory will thank you!

Fifth, creating pictures to remember information is valuable because the mind thinks in pictures. Constructing big pictures with central figures and supporting details also fits the theme of this book. It is important to keep three things in mind when forming these images:

A. Produce action; your brain does not think in stall photographs. The more action there is, the more details you can employ in a scene.

B. Make the picture as crazy and disproportionate as possible. It will be easy to remember the details as you recall the strange or unique things in the picture.

C. Associate the overall theme of the scene with something that will allow you to remember why it is related to the concepts or details found in it.

One of the best mnemonic images that I have created was for the infective organism, chlamydia. Chlamydia is classified between a virus and a bacterium and is responsible for causing at least five ailments:

- Elephantiasis (sever swelling of the leg),
- Lymphogranulareum venereum (a venereal disease),
- Pneumonia,
- Anal Abnormalities, and
- A disease termed parrot fever.

The scene's location is the bottom of the ocean where a large clam is sitting (Chlamydia). On top of the clam stands an elephant (elephantiasis) with Elvie (pronounced LV for lymphogranulareum venereum), an acquaintance of mine, lying on her back, coughing (pneumonia). Now Elvie had a reputation for excessive hip movement, and that is how the association with anal abnormalities is made. Finally, perched on her shoulder is a talkative parrot (parrot fever) who is ready to tell Elvie about any new discoveries that medicine makes with Chlamydia, leaving room to expand the information in the picture when it becomes necessary. I have retained the details of this image for several years and have found this technique a significant aid to my memory.

The last mnemonic method involves finding any connection between information possessed and that which needs to be stored. This can be in the form of combining any of the previous five techniques or by employing number and letter sets. All that is involved in these sets is the recall of the number of items in a group, "Nine stages of hell in Dante's Inferno, and I have only six; must find three more." This technique works even better with long lists broken into lettered groups. Thus, say you have 14 items to remember, but four have the first initial of A, three have a C, and two have an R and S. This is a simple tool, and if you can find these similarities, your work will be easier.

If you have too many sets to remember, this method can be confusing, but combining this method with others will help to alleviate that problem.

It is helpful to begin forming these mnemonics at the first exposure to the material. This allows enough time to find associations. I know that initially it is not always easy to find associations, but usually you can find one or more of the six categories into which you can place the material. Be versatile and use any method that works for you.

The power of mnemonics is in their ability to reduce long, unrelated strings of information into short, related lists. Practice the techniques! If you invest time in training your memory, its work will save you from boring repetition. If you are not having a particularly creative time, however, then repeat the information until you know it. At least with repetition you are being active with the material, and activity is a prerequisite to learning.

This chapter can be summarized with four rules for efficient memorization:

One, concentrate on what you are learning;

Two, process the material internally, ensuring that it fits together in a logical sequence and that you understand it as a whole;

Three, establish a relationship between the material you want to learn and material you already possess – association is necessary;

And **four**, realize that any mental activity performed on material, such as forming pictures, rhymes, or acronyms, increases the depth of processing and automatically helps you to form connections that improve retrievability.

"The Big Picture" Parietal Relations

1. Association is key to memory.

2. Immediate memory is initially processed material and is enhanced by focusing attention on the material to be remembered.

3. Short-term memory is the temporary storage place for information and is enhanced by concentration, grouping, and understanding.

4. Long-term memory is just that – long-term storage of material – and is initially dependent on immediate and short-term memory.

5. Memory usually fails because of: an initial lack of focus, lack of understanding, material not learned in its context, and a lack of motivation.

6. Mnemonics will improve your recall. Learn how to use them to your advantage.

7. Repetition is useful if your associative powers dim.

CHAPTER EIGHT

TWO HEADS ARE BETTER THAN NONE:

STUDYING WITH A PARTNER

Y OU HAVE HEARD THE PROVERB, "TWO HEADS are better than one." Well, I say that two heads are better than none. Often there is "no head" at work trying to learn, assimilate, or memorize information, because you are lost, bogged down, or bored by what you are doing. With two heads working together, you can eliminate most of these problems and make far greater progress. In this chapter I will consider the reasons for studying with another person, his or her selection, and the most effective methods for group study (group here meaning two, or at the most, three).

Why Study With Someone Else?

I have found studying with a partner to be effective for many reasons, the most important ones being: to increase understanding of the material, to get better grades, and to establish strong and lasting friendships (not necessarily in that order). Studying with another person helps to break the monotony of rigorous, solitary study. Simply put, it is usually more fun to have someone suffering with you who can relate to your circumstances, and anything that is fun results in increased time spent on that activity.

Studying together helps to clarify weak areas. If you cannot make sense of the material together, you will need help of your instructor. By sharing your notes, both will be able to: pick up points that you have missed; fill in the gaps in your notes; and come to understand what material was emphasized in class. It is easier to look up questions when two people benefit from the information and can share the information finding chore.

Studying together keeps you from making a bloody mess in your favorite textbook when your nose smashes on it from exhaustion. This obviously will save you time and books. Who has not been too exhausted from studying to even get up for a double ice cream sundae? Come to think of it, I do not think I have ever been that exhausted! Anyway, having a lively, humorous, handsome, gorgeous, or just plain compatible partner sure makes it easier to press on when you want to shove off.

I benefited the most from studying with a partner when:

1. They told me what they perceived were the main thoughts on the subject matter.

2. They told me what they thought the test questions would be, and

3. I compared their thoughts with my own. I was likely to miss several important points, as was my

partner, but by comparing our knowledge and insights, we were able to have a more complete overall picture. Also, it helped to hear information repeated and to answer questions aloud before the exam. Seeing and hearing information improves retention tremendously!

4. The last reason for studying with a partner is that you can see how your partner studies; thus you will be able to incorporate new and different methods into your study arsenal — improving your overall study skills.

The Partner

After you have decided that studying with another person is beneficial, how do you go about finding a good partner? Choose carefully. Here is where you can reap tremendous benefits or really screw up! It is sort of like choosing a mate — two elements are essential: equality and compatibility. In order to do well in this venture, you will spend a lot of time together, so it is important that your time is enjoyable and profitable. You need to find someone of about equal intelligence, speed of comprehension, and style of organization. Otherwise, the person with good study skills becomes an inexpensive tutoring service, which is not the intent of this method.

Spend the first part of the semester studying with different people until you find someone who is compatible with you. Do not jump into a study relationship; it takes time to find the right people, so check out your options. Make sure that you find someone with whom you enjoy working, especially someone in your major field of study. Then you will have more than one course to study together.

It is very important to make sure that your partner is reliable and diligent in the work together. If he or she is chronically ill prepared for your sessions, or has not appeared for the third consecutive study session, it is time to find another partner.

If you cannot find the gorgeous person with the high IQ, do not fret. You will probably do better in the long run. In studying, this philosophy will probably help you keep your mind on your work! Good rationalization goes a long way!

Finally, I suggest studying only with one person at a time and certainly never more that two. Larger groups are for parties and prayer meetings, but not for studying. You will quickly discover, even with three people together, that you will have trouble pacing yourself and will begin to get into a morass of details. Two people works best in a marriage and also when studying together.

Methods for Studying With a Partner

When you are studying with a partner, avoid at all costs getting bogged down in trivia. It will happen if you are not careful. I have found that you can master the big picture and then tie in enough details for the big A, when studying with a partner.

Here is how. First, begin with preparation. Each partner should have a good rewritten set of notes and also have read them once before getting together. When reading your notes and assigned reading material beforehand, observe: the areas that you are missing; areas that you do not understand; and areas that you think are especially important. Come to the study session prepared to give, instruct, and clarify points with your partner. You will leave reinforced and informed. **If you can teach something, you know it.** If you come to the study session as if you were going to teach it, you will then come away with a solid understanding.

Set time limits for your sessions and try to adhere to them. Remember, you probably have other subjects to tackle. Take adequate breaks in your sessions to keep yourself fresh, but remember your purpose and minimize the lengthy gab sessions. Fifty minutes of study, ten minutes for breaks is still a good rule. The achievement of good grades and learning requires fifty minutes per hour.

Now that you and your partner have discussed what you want to accomplish and have a good set of notes and questions in front of you, simply take turns reading aloud, reviewing or questioning your partner on the material in a systematic way. Be sure to leave room for discussion of the misunderstood points. If areas of questions arise, try to answer them quickly. If the answer is not readily available, jot it down to ask the professor, and move on. Get through the material once quickly and decide what needs more work. When going through the subject matter, alternate with each other and be sure that you have gone through all of the material at least twice. The first time you explain the material and ask the questions, and the second time you listen and answer questions.

Devise questions as you go along, trying to second-guess the teacher's exam questions; this is a good study method when studying alone and is enhanced with two heads. Also, when studying together, try to create parietal pictures. As you recall, parietal pictures are crazy and exaggerated mental pictures to aid your memory. Your joint effort will enhance their quality.

All of the other rules and ideas for good study techniques apply when studying together. So do not study in front of the television or on a bed.

After you have covered the material, clarified points, and noted questions for the professor, be sure to re-state the main points and review them. In my study sessions with a partner, one of us would list the major points and facts, so that we would have them for a quick review, and the other person would get a copy of this.

Remember, for most classes your notes are worth 70-75 percent of the grade; so review them diligently and make them more complete with material from the texts.

At the beginning of this chapter, I mentioned that one of the advantages of studying with a partner was the establishment of strong and lasting friendships. I remember the many times I spent studying with someone, especially with two or three very special people. The fellowship and empathy that we shared made those times some of my most precious memories. Always (this time, I mean always) remember that we are relational people, and if we can enhance our study skills and establish positive, reinforcing relationships at the same time, we indeed have a powerful tool.

On the other hand, if just the sound of the other person's voice drives you up the wall, then your study skills will become frazzled, and the only relationship that you will want to make is with quiet. It is your education; find someone whose personality and overall academic skills complement your, and vice versa.

**"The Big Picture" Two Heads
Are Better Than None**

1. Reasons for studying with another person include: increasing your understanding, clarifying information, comparing notes and impressions on the important points, and seeing how our partner studies.

2. Equality and compatibility are the main criteria in choosing a partner.

3. Study with one person at a time; groups larger than two are for parties, not study groups.

4. When studying together: avoid trivia, be prepared for your session, set time limits and stick to them, create test questions and "big picture fact sheets" as you proceed, and examine material quickly at first, and in detail later.

5. The establishment of strong and lasting relationships is an important by-product of studying with a partner.

CHAPTER NINE

GO TO THE SOURCE:

A PRACTICAL APPROACH TO TEACHERS

DURING MY TWENTY-ONE YEARS AS A STUDENT, I HAD many outstanding instructors. One was my pathology professor, who epitomized the essence of inspired teaching. He taught in an organized, concise, interesting, and humorous fashion. He was skilled in making his class presentation pertinent and practical, and he was famous for making dead facts become alive.

This special professor made learning a tough subject enjoyable. He also encouraged close relationships between his students and himself. I remember piling into his car with three other classmates to go a funeral home in Henryetta, Oklahoma, to perform our first autopsy. He was the master pathologist, and by cultivating a close relationship with him, we learned more than just "dead" facts. We began to understand the workings of a superb pathologist's mind in solving medical problems. This has tremendous value. You can get the facts from any good textbook, but you can only see how things are done, firsthand, by observation. Cultivating solid relationships with your faculty is basic to learning more than bare facts.

Many times in this book I have explained why your teachers are such a tremendous resource for you. Among other things, they have many suggestions on how to become a better student. Sadly, their knowledge and expertise on the best ways to study their fields are only minimally tapped by most students. Now I am devoting a full chapter to this topic so you can learn to take full advantage of the student-teacher relationship. This chapter is divided into three sections. Part one deals with the value you can derive from your instructors before the class actually begins. Part two discusses the aspects of a productive student-teacher relationship during the course. Part three deals with interaction you may want to have with the instructor after you have completed a class.

Before the Course Begins

Approaching the teacher before a class begins has obvious value in at least four areas. First, it helps you to establish rapport with the teacher, thereby making you more than just a face without a name in class. This is the first step in establishing a relationship with the teacher. This practice has value even if there are more than a hundred students in a class, because after you have approached an instructor once, the teacher will remember you and you will feel more comfortable approaching him or her again.

Next, you may wonder: "What is this class all about? Do I have adequate prerequisites? How much study time does the professor think will be needed for this course? What sources other than the textbook are helpful?" It is helpful to have these questions answered before the class begins so that you can be better prepared for the class.

The beginning of the course is a good time to get some suggestions from the teacher about how you should approach the subject. This is the teacher's area of expertise so he or she should know the best ways for you to assimilate the material they present. After all, part of the definition of the word "teach" in *Webster's New Collegiate Dictionary* is "to guide the studies of." So let teachers do their job. Let them show you how to study their subjects.

Finally, approaching the instructor before a class begins gives you the advantage of dropping the class early if you find that you are not adequately prepared for it or that it is not what you want. Additionally, you may find that there will be interpersonal problems between you and the professor. If you drop a class three weeks into the semester, it is very hard to replace it with another class. Find out as early as possible if the class you are taking and the person teaching it are what you want and what you can handle.

Attitude and Approach to Teachers

This is a good place to discuss your attitude and approach to your teachers. When approaching your instructors, try to keep four things in mind. First, keep in mind that you have a right to expect certain things from them. It is reasonable to expect profitable, organized, and interesting lectures. The lectures should also have some practical value. Next, it is fair to assume that the instructor's job involves helping you to master the techniques of learning his or her subject. It is also fair to expect to be treated fairly and with dignity during lectures and laboratory sessions, as well as in grading. I know that it is not very dignifying to get a 42 percent on a history exam, but if that was your fault, then "death with dignity" is your responsibility, not the teacher's.

Secondly, in approaching the instructor, try to have a humble and learning spirit. You will find that being considered arrogant or unteachable by your teacher is a disadvantage. Most teachers enter the field because they feel that they have something of value to give to students. If you approach them thinking they are there to support your preconceived ideas or just to give you a good grade, then you will invariably have trouble with them. However, if your attitude is one of respect for the position of the teacher as well as enthusiasm for the subject that he or she is teaching, you will build a profitable relationship.

It is not always possible to be enthusiastic or respectful to teachers, because the 42 percent on the history exam may very well have been the teacher's fault. Poor teaching and unfair tests are common occupational hazards for students. This problem leads into the third part of how to approach instructors. When you have misunderstandings or problems with a professor, approach him or her with a group of students to discuss the grievances.

On the first day of medical school I was randomly chosen by my anatomy professor to chair the BITCHS Committee (which stood for Blatant Indiscretions by Teachers Committed Against Helpless Students). He felt that students needed a collective voice to deal with any class problems. This committee was very productive and operated symbiotically with teachers and students. It was composed of three to four students who were not easily intimidated by the professors and who could present themselves well in a group. Also, they were able to argue well and had a good grasp of the subject matter.

After some objections to the title of the committee, its name was changed to the "Amos" committee. Amos was the prophet in the Old Testament who told the women of Israel that they were fat cows. I know that there were many fat cow experiences in my life as a student. It was best to approach this herd as a group, so as not to be trampled.

As it evolved, the committee served three main purposes. First, it was valuable in giving both positive and negative feedback to the teachers regarding their lectures. It also helped communicate to the teachers whether or not the students understood the material presented in class. Second, after exams the committee would question the validity of certain questions and their answers. This was very productive, because the committee was able to have answers revised or questions deleted, thus raising the curve of the test by more than ten points on several occasions. The last function of the committee was that of reviewer. We sat with different course directors and discussed the overall effectiveness of the class. Teachers view you favorably if you have put forth some effort to understand a concept before you use them as a sounding board to reinforce what you have learned. Conversely, if you do not put forth any effort, expecting the teacher to take you through a concept step by step, the teacher will view you unfavorably. We needed to approach our professors from a standpoint of some knowledge. If we had questions, we tried to research the answers on our own first. If we still did not understand, then we went ahead and asked the teachers.

Student-Teacher Relationships during the Course

In discussing the aspects of a productive student-teacher relationship during a course, I will touch upon four major areas: questioning, notes, tests, and ways of enhancing the relationship.

As I have mentioned throughout the book, asking questions and dialoguing are integral parts of the learning process.

You should continually cultivate these skills. Your approach to the professor is of utmost importance in this regard. Doing your part by researching material you do not understand is crucial to having any meaningful dialogue on the questions you have.

During a course, the first question to ask yourself is, "Why am I taking this course, and how will it enhance my educational goals?" Since the professor has probably had many years of training on the subject, he should be able to give you a good answer. If you did not talk to the professor before the class began, this is a good time to ask questions about how to approach the subject matter. If you need a certain grade in the class, this is the appropriate time to ask the instructor how to get it. The more information you have at the beginning of the class, the better chance you have of achieving your goals.

The more you approach a teacher with well-thought out and researched questions, the more he or she will be able to help you assimilate the material in a course. Use the time before and after class, as well as the teacher's office hours. Students who say they can never talk to the teacher usually are not trying very hard. Remember, they are the best source of help to you in learning the subject matter, so go to them with your questions.

If you have the backup of a BITCHS or Amos-type committee, that's great. If not, you should still approach the processor with questions or feedback that you might have. By all means, if you have a question on a test that you have taken, challenge (after researching) the answer that the professor keyed as the right one. I used to pray that God would help me get the right answers to the questions on a test. I learned from experience, however, to pray for the answer that the professor thought was right. These were not always the same.

As I suggested in a previous chapter, try to get a copy of the teacher's lecture notes before the lecture. This will give you valuable information on what is important and help you avoid writer's cramp during the lecture. It will also give you the assurance of having complete notes and even help you organize your notes. Do not neglect this valuable source of information. Even if the teacher will not let you copy his or her notes, you still will gain from the interaction by demonstrating to the instructor your interest and desire to do well in his or her class.

Regarding tests, it is wise to have as much information on them as possible. Most teachers will gladly tell you what they expect from you on tests and will give you many helpful clues on how to prepare. So give yourself a break. Try to get as much information on the content of the exams as the instructor will give you.

Teachers Are People Too

We are all relational beings and need to interact on a human level. Spend time getting to know your professors beyond the classroom. Get to know their backgrounds, their interests, their professional and personal goals, etc. We learn from their lives as well as from the lecture material. This is especially true if the teacher's expertise is in a discipline or field you might enter. You will cherish the relationships you develop with teachers long after you have forgotten 80 percent of the details they gave you in class!

Finally, relationships with your teachers will be valuable to you in the future when you need letters of recommendation. This certainly is not the most important reason for establishing lasting relationships with faculty, but you will probably need these letters, and it is very best to get them from teachers who know you and like you.

After the Fact

When the class is nearing its end, or is finished, you have three major responsibilities. First you have the responsibility of evaluating the class honestly for the benefit of future students. This gives the teacher valuable feedback on his or her performance. It has been my experience that teachers are genuinely interested in students' suggestions for improvement. Students are generally too kind in their evaluations, not wanting to hurt the instructor's feelings or not wanting to jeopardize their grade or recommendation. It does no good, and it is even harmful, to rate a class better than it was. If your honesty will affect your grade or recommendation, then turn it in anonymously, or wait until after the grades are posted to return it. This is your way of grading the professor—see how it feels!

Second, you have the responsibility of getting letters of recommendation for your future use. These are best written right after you have taken a course. The professor knows you and your work, and will be able to write a more personal letter for you. The first step in obtaining this letter is to ask professors (the more the better) if they would each write you a positive letter of recommendation. If someone hedges, let him or her off the hook. You do not want noncommittal letters. If the teacher agrees, ask for a copy of the letter so that you can read it and decide whether or not you want to use it. Finally, ask the professor to keep it on file so that when you need it, he or she can simply print it out on the school or university letterhead, sign it, and send it. Letters of recommendation carry more weight when they come directly from your professor with a recent date as opposed to being a copy of an old letter that you have on file.

Your third responsibility after the class is completed is to get the best possible grade in it. Some people say that you shouldn't be concerned with grades, that they are not a true measure of your knowledge. College and graduate school admissions boards, however, are keenly aware of your grades and use them to compare you with thousands of other applicants. If you can get a better grade, it is certainly worth a try.

The extra effort is especially helpful if you are on the borderline between an A, B, or C. I have successfully used two arguments for getting higher grades in borderline situations. The first one involved my need for the grade, due to the competitiveness of my major or career goals. If it is possible and fair, most teachers want to see their students become successful. So if they can, in good conscience, give you the higher grade, they will. The second argument involved gently but persuasively pointing out the injustice of giving someone with an 89.2 percent average a B, while giving the same B to someone with an 80.1 percent average. Obviously, this does not always work, as illustrated in a *Peanuts* cartoon I once read. In it Peppermint Patty wonders out loud to her teacher how the letter D by itself is a wonderful, important, and dignified letter. "When a minus is put in front of it," she argues, "it loses its dignity, appears drained, and has lost its power and strength." Her teacher would not change her grade, but promised that if she was ever on trial for her life, she would want Peppermint Patty for her lawyer.

If you never try to raise your grade or seem concerned about it, the professor will assume that grades are not important to you and he or she will not feel bad about giving you the lower of a borderline grade. If, however, you make your desires known to your teachers, they will at least give your request some thought. This practice can make a significant difference in your grade point average. If you never try to talk a policeman out of a ticket, then you will always simply take what he or she gives you. But if you try to talk your way out of a ticket, you might have a 20 percent chance of succeeding. Over a lifetime, that is significant. The same is true of your G.P.A.

I opened this chapter by writing about a superb pathology professor. I will close by telling you about another professor I had. This instructor was similar to the first one in that his lectures were organized, practical, and interesting. He also encouraged close relationships with his students and served as a role model and mentor to many of us. He was secure enough to share with us some of his shortcomings, and how he learned from the mistakes he had made in his career. He hoped to help us avoid some of the pain that accompanies mistakes. He also taught us that there is more to us than our studies. To be happy and fulfilled, we need to cultivate other areas of our lives that have value, such as our family and social relationships, our physical well being, and our intellectual and cultural growth. He taught us from his knowledge and from his life, and that gift of himself was more valuable than any other source of information available.

"The Big Picture" Go To The Source

1. There are many advantages to cultivating relationships with your professors.

2. Approach your instructors before a course begins to establish rapport with them, have questions answered, learn how to approach the class, and drop the class early if it is not suitable for you.

3. A student's attitude toward teachers should include expecting quality lectures, getting help from them, and being treated with dignity.

4. Students should approach teachers with a humble and teachable spirit, come to them with a group when trouble arises, and ask most questions only after you have tried to research them on your own.

5. During a course, the professor will be able to answer your questions, guide your study and note taking, and provide necessary information for upcoming exams.

6. Responsibilities you have as the class is finishing include evaluating it honestly, asking for letters of recommendation, and discussing your grade if it is important to you.

CHAPTER TEN

PRESSURIZE YOUR CABIN:

PREPARING FOR AND TAKING TEST

PRESSURE HAS LONG BEEN KNOWN TO HAVE strange effects on people, especially students. The pressure of exams is one of the most severe tests of a student's ability to cope under stress. Students have been know to completely buckle during strenuous times, doing very crazy things like staying awake three nights in a row before an exam to cram sixty pages of math theorems and formulas that they have never seen before; popping pills; eating coffee grounds to keep their eyes open long enough to memorize the number of ribs on a female catfish; or, on the morning of the exam, blankly staring at a set of notes taken three weeks before and swearing they have never seen them before in their lives.

There is no doubt that, for most students, test time is an anxious period filled with certain unavoidable pressures. The trick is to have the extra adrenalin and pressure work for you rather than against you. You can either let the excess energy help motivate you to prepare adequately for your upcoming task or let it feed your delusions that somehow God well send an angel to dictate the test answers to you.

This chapter is about regulating pressure under the load of exams. It has been said on more than one occasion that I received a high mark on an exam because of my skill at taking exams, not because of my knowledge. I think some of those comments might have been derogatory, but I took them as a compliment. If a B student operates at an A level on exams, he or she will open more doors and have more choices for his or her future goals.

Unfortunately, the opposite is more often true. Students who know the material well often get a lower grade on an exam because of poor test-taking skills, not because their knowledge is lacking. Knowing the material well is only part of being a good test-taker. There are certain definable, proven skills for test preparation, taking the test, alleviating test anxiety, and reviewing exams once they are graded.

Much of this book has been geared toward preparing you for exams, so you will find some repetition in this chapter. However, as someone once said, "Repetition is the mother of learning." I guess I did not repeat his name enough. Just kidding! It was John Paul Richter in 1807. So, here we go.

Preparations for Exams

I have divided the first section on preparation for exams into four parts: 1.) several weeks before the exam; 2.) several days before the exam; 3.) the day before the exam; and 4.) the day of the exam.

Several Weeks before the Exam

The first thing to do when starting a new unit is to **set up a study schedule** that will allow you enough time to learn the material adequately. The time to begin preparing for the next exam is at the beginning of the unit. I tried to arrange my study schedule so that I would be ready to take the exam three days before it was actually given. This gave me the opportunity, right before the exam, to study with a partner and get his or her insights, ask the professor any questions I still had, and leave my overall study schedule intact. This kept me from abandoning my other classes and study schedules just to get ready for this one test. It also kept me from neglecting everything else that was going on in my life at the time. Even though this did not always work, I aimed for this kind of sanity to keep me from being boiled in the midnight oil.

Next, **study in units** that are organized and concise. This will give you an advantage during review because you will know how much material you have covered and how much is left to tackle. Also do **periodic overall reviews**. Once a week, briefly review all of the material in a particular section. Doing this will dramatically speed up review time right before the exam, because the material will be fresh in your mind, and you will have assimilated more of it.

Also make sure that you **have a complete set of lecture notes**, as I mentioned earlier. Again, 70 to 75 percent of the test questions come directly from the lecture material. Remember to recopy your notes soon after class to complete them, make them neater and easier to read, and to give you more exposure to them. I recopied my notes faithfully throughout college and medical school. This technique served me well in many classes.

In addition, I recommend that you keep a separate list of **test questions that you create**. I discussed earlier the advantage of devising your own questions. Briefly, it helps you be more active in your studies, while teaching you how to select important concepts and facts in your study material. If you keep a record of these facts, they will be helpful during your review.

Likewise, it is helpful to **keep a "big picture" fact sheet**. On this fact sheet place only the major concepts and their supporting facts, along with any formulas or key words that you would find useful in a very quick review. This sheet would never total more than three to four pages in length. It was very useful for a one- to two-hour review, and it was ideal for studying right before the exam.

Finally, at least one week before the exam, ask the professor four things: what **specific topics** are going to be covered on the exam; what material will be **emphasized** on the test; what **type of questions** will be on the test (this often will give you important clues on how to prepare for the exam); and what **clues** the professor can give you when preparing for the test. Many teachers are willing to guide students in their review for exams. It is smart to find out as much as possible about the exam directly from the teacher.

Several Days before the Exam

This is the pressure-cooker time for most students, but if you follow a few, simple principles, you can harness the steam to help your brain work more efficiently. First, study effectively with a partner. As I have discussed, this will help you have the motivation and stamina for review, while giving you another perspective on the exam material. This time can also be used for clarifying questionable material with someone else as a sounding board to measure your understanding of it.

Attend the classes right before the exam. Many students think that this is the time to skip class to get in a few extra hours of study. During the last few class sessions before an exam, however, the teacher usually gives important information about the upcoming test. Also, if new material is presented in class, you want to hear it. Getting new material close to the test also means that it is fresher in your mind and therefore easier to remember for the test. Remember, your best source for exams is your lecture notes, so go to class to the end and take notes.

Continue to revise and update your "big picture" fact sheet. If you get bogged down in the details while reviewing your notes for a test, go to the big picture of what you are studying. If you are trying to nail facts onto a flimsy base, your knowledge will become broken or splintered. If, however, you have a solid foundation for the main ideas, you can better understand the supporting facts.

Finally, harness the cram monster and make it work for you. Many educators will tell you that cramming before an exam reveals poor study habits. I disagree. Cramming is worthwhile and, if used correctly, can dramatically increase your test score. The trick is to use cramming for review, not first exposure. If you are cramming material that you have never seen before, you will find yourself in big trouble.

Intensive study of material that has been at least partially assimilated, however, will increase your short-term retention of it and thus help you on the exam. Many studies have shown that the major factor in retention for exams is recentness of exposure to the material. So cram what you know. You will learn it better and remember it longer.

If you do find yourself in the position of cramming new material just before an exam, here are a few hints to help you weather the inevitable storm. First, make sure that you know the lecture notes. Second, read the chapter introductions, topic sentences, graphs, italicized words; and, more importantly, read the chapter summaries. Third, try to get a copy of old exams to see what material the professor emphasized. Again, reviewing old test is a good idea even if you know the material. Finally, if possible, get a review book that gives you just the bare facts and study that.

The Day before the Exam

I have always used the day before the exam for an overall, quick review of the material, using my notes and "big picture" fact sheet. I tried to review these at least twice, once to learn what areas still needed polishing and once to expose myself to the material one more time.

Many people will tell you to get a full night's sleep before the exam, even if you are not finished with your review. They argue that this will help you be refreshed and have a clear mind for the exam. That is hogwash! First of all, if you have not finished studying, you will be too uptight to sleep. Second, I have not been able to find any studies to confirm the idea that losing a few hours of sleep will make you lose something you once knew. And third, there are many studies that suggest that your body produces increased amounts of adrenalin during stressful periods, enabling your brain to function adequately for longer periods of time. If you do not have the material secured, stay up and tie it down. Remember, recentness of exposure is one of the most important contributors to good short-term memory.

It is evident throughout this book that I advocate a systematic, scheduled approach to study, that includes getting a full night's sleep before an exam. But, there will be times when that is just not possible. Be flexible, and do what needs to be done the day before the test.

The Day of the Exam

It is a good idea to have something to eat before the exam, but do not "pig out." Doing so will sap your energy as the blood flow shifts from your brain to your stomach. If the test is going to be an extended affair, bring a candy bar or bag of peanuts into the exam room with you.

Arrive a few minutes before the exam begins with extra paper and writing materials. If you arrive too early, you will just have more time to get anxious. If you are late, you will have missed the instructions. This will put you at a disadvantage from the start as your anxiety level goes through the roof!

Stay away from large groups of classmates right before the exam. "Nervous Nellie" will invariably bring up a picky detail that you have not studied (and which the teacher has probably never heard of it), increasing your anxiety level even more.

Finally, when you go into the exam room, try to find a seat that is as far away from distractions as possible. Usually this means not sitting in the front row, near doors or windows, or near a noisy test-taker. I remember my first anatomy exam. I thought it would be a good idea to sit next to my best friend, so that we could give each other emotional support. But, to my shock and distraction, he was the loudest test taker in the state of Oklahoma. His pencil blazed loudly across the test, and he breathed as though he was nourishing his brain with oxygen the way a engineer would feed his locomotive with coal. We stayed best of friends in medical school, but that was partially because I didn't have to sit near him again during exams.

The Examination

In dealing with the mechanics of test taking, I will first list some generalizations that I have found helpful. Then I will cover the methods for answering essay as well as objective questions.

Generalizations

First, look over the test to determine the number and type of questions. Then determine the approximate time you have per question and divide your time appropriately.   Next, read the test instructions. They may tell you that you only have to answer a certain percentage of the questions on the test.

Answer the questions that you know first. This will ensure that you get credit for what you know if you run out of time. If you are unsure about any questions, mark them and return to them later. Remember that another question later in the test may give you valuable information for an earlier one.

Answer questions as you think the teacher would have you answer them. Remember, the teacher's answer is not always the same as the true answer.

Take questions at their face value. Do not read anything into questions. Concentrate on the rule, not the exception, in any given situation. Most teachers want tests to be straightforward and are not interested in the death penalty for your test grade.

If you have a question about some aspect of the test, ask the professor about it during the exam. If the professor does not want to answer the question, he or she will tell you. Most professors, however, will clear up confusing points for you.

Finally, fight the tendency to finish quickly. There is no correlation between those students who finish first and those who do the best on a test. Work until you are satisfied that you have answered all of the questions to the best of your ability.

Essay Questions

Essay questions are usually the hardest to answer, because the teacher does not provide you with a choice of answers to jog your memory. If you keep six principles in mind when answering essay questions, however, you will find them less troublesome.

One, read the question slowly, underlining key words and phrases as you do. This will help you determine exactly what the question is asking and the type of answer the teacher wants. Pay attention to length restrictions to answers as well.

Two, organize your answer before you write it, using the words and organization presented in the question. Outline the different points that you need to make, incorporating introductory and summary statements. This will prevent the answer from being a random set of facts.

Three, start with general statements that you then support with facts and examples, which will further help the organization of your answer. Such a presentation will be appreciated by the professor who will likely spend most of his or her time wading through swamps of unorganized essay answers.

Four, when you are sure of the answer, be concise and write only what is requested. When you need to fake an answer, write as much as you can on all of the topics that you feel relate to the question. Hopefully, the teacher will find something of value in your answer to warrant some points. Always write something! You will not get any points for questions left blank, but you may pick up one half to three-quarters credit on faked answers.

Five, be conscious of time restrictions. It is very easy when writing lengthy answers to lose track of time, so keep your watch on you desk to remind you to budget you time.

Six, review you work to make sure that you have adequately answered the question. Also check your grammar and spelling, if you have time.

Objective Questions

When given a choice, I would rather take an objective test any day. This is because the answer is usually provided for you in the question, and all you need to do is to match the information given with that stored in the parietal lobes of you brain. I will list the strategies that I have found helpful in answering multiple choice, matching, and true-false questions.

One, read the question slowly and answer quickly. If you are in doubt, answer with your first impression. This allows your subconscious mind to play a role in answering the question.

Two, beware of universal statements; they are almost always wrong because in academics there are very few universal truths. Universal statements contain words like always, never, no, non, all, every, and most.

Three, use a notation system to keep track of your thinking during the test. I use T (true), PT (partially true), F (false), and PF (partially false) to indicate my impression of a statement. This helps me to separate the different choices and decreases the need for backtracking. This system is also very helpful for questions that contain "all of the above" or "none of the above" alternatives. When you are not sure of an answer, consider only those you have marked with a T or PT. This will increase your odds of getting the answer right.

Four, when you are unsure of an answer, here are a few tips:

1. The most general answer tends to be the correct one

2. The longest answer option is often the correct one

3. Repetition of the question in the answer often indicates that the answer is true

4. If two opposite options are offered, one of these is usually the correct answer

5. Choose true instead of false, because negative alternatives are harder to write well or convincingly

6. If the answer is a number, the correct answer is often a middle value, so eliminate the highest and lowest options

7. In blind guessing, choose the same option throughout, usually B or C.

*Remember, these are only tips, not "hard and fast" rules. Knowledge is your best guide.

Five, many people will tell you not to change answers when rereading the test. Statistically, however, answers that are changed tend to be correct. If you have good reason for changing an answer, do it. If not, then stay with your first impression.

Six, avoid looking for runs or patterns of true/false or multiple-choice questions. There is usually not an even distribution in the answer key.

Seven, use the process of elimination for matching. Match those you know first, then select the rest from a reduced set of options.

Eight, when solving a problem, work out your answer before looking at the possible options. This will eliminate bias in your work. Also, save tough problems for last, unless they have a disproportionate amount of credit.

If you follow these strategies, your test scores will increase significantly. Remember, there are skills for learning, but there are also skills for communicating what you know on test.

Test Anxiety

The best way to alleviate exam jitters is to be prepared for the exam. For most people, the level of anxiety before and during the exam correlates inversely with the amount of time spent and the efficiency of that time, i.e. the more time and efficiency, the less anxiety.

I have treated several patients who had severe anxiety and who performed far below their level of competence as a result of it. I was taught a simple hypnotic technique to counteract test anxiety by Donald Schafer, M.D., of the University of California, Irvine. This technique has worked well for my patients and will likely work for you, if you diligently follow these simple steps. First, close your eyes and concentrate on your breathing for a few minutes. Let it become slower, deeper, and more regular. Then imagine yourself, comfortable and relaxed, at the place where you usually study. After you do this, pick up a pen or pencil—whichever you will use on the test— and suggest to yourself that when you do this just as the test begins, you will feel as comfortable as you do sitting in your study chair at home, or wherever you study. Repeat this suggestion several times, and let it work for you during exams.

If it does not work for you during the test, then try closing your eyes and taking three slow, deep breathes. Take a minute to try to imagine a relaxing scene like sitting on the beach or sitting near a warm fire in winter. This method often has a relaxing effect.

After the Exam

After your test is graded and handed back to you, you have three responsibilities. First, you need to go over the exam and note what questions you missed and why you missed them. This is a helpful, although painful, way to learn.

Second, you have the responsibility of getting the best grade possible. If you have questions that are marked wrong and you disagree with the keyed answer, then talk to your professor about it. Be prepared. Teachers will often change answers for students, but only if students can persuasively defend their choice of another answer.

Finally, if you notice that some of the questions are written in an ambiguous fashion, tactfully bring them to the teacher's attention. Most teachers welcome this kind of feedback. Doing this may help your grade and keep future students from having to deal with the same poorly written or confusing test questions.

In conclusion, here is a sample test so you can practice the test-taking techniques you have learned in this chapter. I received this test in my sophomore year of college during a philosophy course.

> **Instructions:** Read each question carefully. Answer all questions. Time limit is four hours. Begin immediately.

> **History:** Describe the history of the papacy from its origins to the present day, concentrating especially, but not exclusively, on its social, political, economic, religious, and philosophical impact on Europe, Asia, America, and Africa. Be brief, concise, and specific.

Medicine: You have been provided with a razor blade, a piece of gauze, and a bottle of Scotch. Remove your appendix. Do not suture until your work has been inspected. You have fifteen minutes.

Public Speaking: 2,500 riot-crazed aborigines are storming the classroom. Calm them. You may use any ancient language, except Latin or Greek.

Biology: Create life. Estimate the differences in subsequent human culture if this form of life had developed 500 million years earlier, with special attention to its probable effect on the English Parliamentary System. Prove you thesis.

Music: Write a piano concerto. Orchestrate and perform it with flute and drum. You will find a piano under your seat.

Psychology: Based on your knowledge of their works, evaluate the emotional stability, degree of adjustment and repressed frustrations of each of the following: Alexander of Aphrodisians, Ramseo II, Gregory of Nicea, and Hammurabi. Support your evaluation with quotations from each man's work. Make appropriate references. It is not necessary to translate.

Sociology: Estimate the sociological problems that might accompany the end of the world. Construct an experiment to test your theory.

Management Science: Define management. Define science. How do they relate? Why? Create a generalized algorithm to optimize all managerial decisions. Assuming 370/168 computer supporting 50 on-line terminals, design the communication interface and all necessary control programs to activate your algorithm from each terminal.

Engineering: The disassembled parts of a high-powered rifle have been placed in a box on your desk. You will find an instruction manual, printed in Swahili, next to the box. In ten minutes, a hungry Bengal tiger will be admitted into the room. Take whatever action you feel appropriate. Be prepared to justify your decision.

Economics: Develop a realistic plan for refinancing the national debt. Trace the possible effects of your plan in the following areas: cubism, the Donatist controversy, and the wave theory of light. Outline a method for preventing these effects. Criticize this method from all points of view as demonstrated in your answer to the last question.

Political Science: There is a red telephone on the desk beside you. Start World War III. Report at length on its socio-political effects, if any.

Epistemology: Take a position for or against truth. Prove the validity of your position.

Physics: Explain the nature of matter. Include in your answer an evaluation of the impact of the development of mathematics on science.

Philosophy: Sketch the development of human thought. Estimate its significance. Compare with the development of any other kind of thought.

General Knowledge: Describe in detail. Be objective and specific.

Chemistry: You will be given one pound of lead. Convert it into gold. Return it to the instructor with the experimental procedure.

Mathematics: If X equals p times r squared, construct a formula showing how long it would take a fire ant to drill a hole through a dill pickle, if the length-girth ratio of the ant to the pickle were 98.17 to 1.

Extra Credit: Define the universe. Give three examples.

"The Big Picture" Pressurizing Your Cabin

1. Several weeks before the exam, establish a study schedule, study in units, engage in periodic overall reviews, have a complete set of notes and "big picture" fact sheet, and be sure to ask the instructor about the content of the test.

2. Several days before the exam, study with a partner, go to class, and cram for review, not first exposure. When you need to cram new material, know your notes and chapter summaries and secure old exams.

3. The day before the exam, eat moderately, arrive for the test a few minutes early, stay away from large groups of classmates, and find a seat away from distractions.

4. Test-taking generalizations: Quickly overview the test, read instructions, answer the questions you know first, answer as you think the professor would, take questions at their face value, focus on the rule not exceptions to the rule, fight the impulse to finish quickly.

5. In answering essay questions, read the questions slowly, organize your answers, work from the general to the specific, be concise when you know an answer and lengthy when you do not, always write something, be conscious of your time, and review your work.

6. In answering objective questions, read the question slowly, answer quickly, look for and avoid universal statements, use a notation system, use the odds for questions if you do not know the answer, and change answers for good reasons-otherwise go with your first impressions.

7. Alleviate test anxiety by being prepared and utilizing relaxation techniques.

8. After the exam has been graded, review it to see why you missed certain questions, discuss disagreements with the professor from a standpoint of knowledge, and give the professor feedback on the test.

CHAPTER ELEVEN

LETTING YOURSELF OUT:

WRITING AND SPEAKING SKILLS

IN THE SPRING OF MY JUNIOR YEAR IN COLLEGE, I was required to write twelve papers, three of them term papers. My ethics professor assigned six papers, one due every two weeks. I remember being frustrated in that class because I would get my papers back from the professor without any of his personal comments on them. Only the grade appeared in the upper right-hand corner. I wanted feedback on my work and was beginning to wonder whether my professor was reading my papers at all. So, in my fifth paper I inserted a phrase at the bottom of the fourth page in the middle of a paragraph that read, "If you are still reading this, I will buy you a milkshake." In the margin he wrote, "Make it chocolate." It was his only comment on the entire paper!

Writing is a skill that will not only serve you well in high school and in college, but throughout your life. Being able to write well will open many doors for you professionally. Being able to speak well in public is also a valuable skill that many employers want you to have.

This chapter is about letting yourself out in writing and speaking. I have chosen to group these skills together because of the many similarities between writing a paper and writing a speech. At the end of the chapter I will discuss certain techniques for enhancing the delivery of speeches. There are many good books on writing and speaking effectively, so I will limit my comments to a few pertinent points that I have found helpful in my own academic and professional career.

Writing Papers or Speeches

Writing papers or speeches will be easier if you consistently follow these eight steps: schedule your time, choose a topic, narrow it down, do the research, make an outline, discuss your ideas, write the paper, and revise your work.

Schedule Your Time

Meeting deadlines is an essential part of everyone's life and especially important in writing papers or speeches. Many professors lower your grade for late papers. If your speech is not written in time for you to practice it, you will feel very nervous when you present it. As soon as you get the assignment, prepare a reasonable schedule around the remaining seven steps: choosing your topic, narrowing it down, making an outline, etc. You will save yourself many hours of lost sleep the few nights before the assignments are due. This system is helpful unless, of course, you cherish those times without sleep or feel the need to do what everyone else is doing, procrastinating, so that you will be accepted by your peers.

Choosing a Topic

When choosing a topic for a paper or for a speech, try to write either about things familiar to you or things that interest you. Such topics give you the opportunity to share your knowledge or acquire new knowledge Even though some professors will assign papers on "The Theological Significance of the Death of Bubbles the Hippo," most of the time you have a choice of topics. So write with you heart and mind together.

Try to stay away from abstract subjects. In general, people want to read or hear about things that affect their daily lives like: How to get a date in class, the best strategies for paying less taxes, and how to get better grades while studying less.

When choosing a topic, realize that it's difficult to pick something that has never been written or spoken about previously. As King Solomon wrote in the book of Ecclesiastes, "What has been will be again, what has been done will be done again; there is nothing new under the sun." This is a good insight. You can try to choose topics that are new and interesting to your audience. When that's not possible, you can choose a new and interesting way to present a familiar topic.

Narrow It Down

After you have selected a topic, make sure that it is narrow enough to handle in a five hundred-word essay, ten-minute speech, or whatever the assignment is. If the topic is too broad, like "The Development of Human Thought and Its Significance for the Twenty-First Century," you will spend the whole paper or speech on generalities, unable to say anything specific or practical. If you are not sure if the topic is too broad, ask your professor for guidance. The big picture in writing and speaking is not in lengthy dissertations that have little to say, but in the organized, concise outline and presentation of your ideas.

Research

Researching the paper or speech can be profitable and time-efficient, or it can be unproductive and ulcerogenic (causing ulcers). The first thing to do is have the big picture of the narrow topic in mind. Then you need to be aware of the research sources that are available to you. Obviously, your best source will be Internet search engines or the school or public library. If you do not know how to use them well, close this book now and get your body and mind over to one of them. Then ask the librarian to show you how to take advantage of this most valuable resource.

Encyclopedias are valuable because they often give extensive outlines and several reference sources on any given subject. The index of Periodical Literature—articles in magazines—is useful, too. An often overlooked source, it gives the most recent information on most topics.

When researching a topic, take voluminous notes. The more information you have in front of you when writing the paper or speech, the easier it will be to compile it. Also, keep a bibliography on the sources that you have used. This will save you time if you need to refer to them again.

The Outline

After you have researched the topic and taken adequate notes, make an extensive outline of the paper or speech. Your outline is the big picture of the paper or speech. If you put sufficient thought and effort into the outline, you will not have to spend time rewriting the paper because you do not like the way it is organized.

Having an extensive outline will also decrease the time it takes to write the manuscript, because you will be less prone to writer's block. You will have the road map so that you know where you have been, where you are, and where you are going.

Discuss Your Ideas

After you have made an outline, it is a good idea to discuss it with a friend or with the teacher. They can give you valuable ideas and feedback on it. The time to have the work reviewed is after you have made the outline, not after you have finished your paper or speech. At this stage it is still easy to make major revisions. After the paper or speech is finished, it is not only more difficult and time-consuming to make changes, but it is also more disheartening and ego deflating.

Pick someone to review your work who believes in you and whom you trust with your feelings. You will be more likely to believe and accept any negative criticism that he or she might give you.

Writing the Paper or Speech

Writing the first draft of the paper or speech is actually the easiest part of the process if you have chosen an interesting topic, have kept its scope narrow, have sufficiently researched and outlined it, and have discussed it with someone you respect. When writing the first draft, let the ideas flow onto the paper. You will have time later to correct the grammar and punctuation. Just get the ideas onto the paper for the first writing. A simple rule to follow in writing or speaking is to first tell your readers/audience what you plan to say, say it, then tell them what you have said. This will give the material an organized appearance and also reinforce major points.

When writing, try to keep in mind five simple concepts:

1. Say only one thing at a time and keep the arguments, examples, and contributory ideas pertinent to the topic.

2. Ensure that the sentences have continuity and that the ideas flow comfortably together.

3. Be as clear as possible. If you wish to make a point, be certain you have made it. Clear writing indicates clear thinking.

4. Do not use extra words or examples. Be as concise as possible to promote clarity.

5. Use humor in writing. If a point can be made in a funny or humorous way, it has a better chance of being remembered, and it will also keep the audience's attention focused on your paper or speech.

Revise Your Work

Revising your paper or speech can be as time-consuming as writing the first draft. This is the time to improve sentence structure, correct punctuation, and ensure that the ideas flow in a logical sequence. This is usually not as interesting as writing the first draft, but if you take your time, the paper or speech will take on a professional appearance, and the mechanics will not distract from the information you are trying to convey.

Concerning Public Speaking

After a paper is finished, you turn it in, but after you have finished writing a speech, your work is only half over. The most grueling part for many people is to get up in front of a group of other people and give the speech. I know this is true, because I used to get the feeling of having a herd of angry mosquitoes (most people get butterflies—I get mosquitoes) in the pit of my stomach as I was about to deliver a speech. At the beginning of my speech, my voice would betray me and sound as though someone were slowly letting the air squeak out of a balloon. I was really quite painful to listen to, I'm sure.

After being on two college speech teams and being president of the last one, I learned several helpful strategies for overcoming my fear of speaking. One, as I've said, is to speak on a familiar topic or one that you find interesting. If you do, you will have a special interest in sharing the material and more likely give a successful speech.

The second strategy is to make sure you have a well-written speech. If you feel good about what you are going to present, you will feel excited about delivering it.

Third, practice your speech in front of friends, mirrors, or a video camera. If you know how you look or have feedback as you are presenting the speech, you can adjust your posture and gestures until you feel and look comfortable. Practicing like this gives you the sense of being in front of a live audience. If the image in the mirror walks away or falls asleep, you know that you're in trouble.

The fourth, fifth, and sixth strategies are . . . practice, practice, practice! The more familiar you are with your subject, the less chance you will panic. Even though you wrote the speech, you need to review it as much as possible, so that if you do start to panic, you will not blank on its contents.

Carry notes with you, even if you feel ready to deliver your speech from memory. This gives you the assurance that if you completely black on your presentation, you can quickly find your place in your notes and proceed. Remember, life insurance is for peace of mind, not immediate use. Notes are good insurance!

In memorizing a speech, keep the outline of it uppermost in your mind. The big picture is very helpful here. If you know where you have been in your speech, where you are, and where you are going, you might black on a few words, but you can always move to the next major point.

Finally, in delivering a speech, be enthusiastic! Realize that speaking is a tool that allows you to share yourself with others.

The key to this whole chapter is practicing your writing and speaking skills. Experience improves quality and confidence, and the result can be rewarding—perhaps even fun!

"The Big Picture" Letting Yourself Out

1. Writing and speaking well will serve you all of your life.

2. In writing papers or speeches, follow eight steps: prepare a reasonable time schedule; choose a topic familiar or interesting to you; narrow the topic; research your presentation; outline your work; discuss the outline with a professor or friend; and tell the audience what you plan to say, say it, then review what you said.

3. In writing, keep five concepts in mind: say one thing at a time; write with continuity; be as clear as possible; be concise; and use humor when appropriate.

4. When speaking, be interested in your topic; have a well written manuscript; practice the speech in front of friends, the mirror, etc.; practice, practice, practice; carry notes with you; and memorize the outline of the speech first.

5. Be enthusiastic! The more you write or speak, the more you will improve, and the easer it will be.

CHAPTER TWELVE

WRAPPING THE PRESENT

The Big Picture

THIS BOOK IS DESIGNED TO BE A PRESENT THAT you give to yourself. The contents are as follows: better grades, more comprehensive knowledge, and better utilization of your time. But obviously the results are up to you. If you use this gift, i.e. practice the principles contained herein and approach your studies with an enthusiastic attitude, you will be very satisfied. However, if you neglect to use your gift, i.e. neglect to change bad habits and patterns or lack perseverance in your studies, you will be setting yourself up for disappointment.

Realize at the outset that you are primarily responsible for your success. Do not fall into the trap of blaming others or circumstances for your failures. This is a dangerous habit, because you are admitting to a loss of control over your life, and if you are not in control of yourself, who is?

This chapter is intended to finish the wrapping of your present by placing a splendid bow on it. The end of this book will show you that developing "your other sides" and sowing healthy seeds will strengthen your overall abilities as a student and as a person is key to your success.

Everyone realizes there is more to life than just being a student, but if you are not careful, you will find yourself engaged only in studying or activities related to studying. When this happens, you will forfeit the necessary education offered by the other areas of you life. Decide at the outset what place studies will have in your world, and do not let them dominate you. You will be more "educated" if you take care of your body, establish solid relationships, and cultivate outside interests in addition to studying.

Your Physical Side

Be extremely cautious about neglecting your physical health. Your body is the instrument of learning, and it must be well tended. There are many studies suggesting that regular exercise augments mental stamina, while creating an increased sense of self-confidence. Exercise increases the production of endorphins in your body. Endorphins are chemicals your body produced naturally that, among other things, add to your sense of well-being. Increasing your mental stamina and self-confidence will help you study better.

Your body also needs a balanced diet to operate at peak efficiency. How do you know if you are eating right? Simple, be sure that your diet contains adequate, but not excessive, nutrients s from the four basic food groups: 1) low–fat or non-fat dairy products; 2) lean meat, fish, or poultry; 3) breads, cereals, or grains; and 4) fruits and vegetables.

Being overweight will cause your body to divert energy from you brain cells to feed your fat cells. You ideal body weight is also your peak brainpower weight. Take care of your body if you want it to perform at your best. Enough said!

Your Relational Side

So much satisfaction and fulfillment in life comes from your relationships with other people. If you neglect this aspect of your life because of your studies you are cheating yourself. You learn valuable, practical lessons from every relationship. It is to your advantage to cultivate the relationships that are most important to you.

Using your studies to avoid meaningful relationships will ultimately cut you off from some of the greatest experiences in life. Of course, some relationships can be as full of pain as pleasure, but few people reach their full potential without the growth that comes from all kinds of significant human relationships. As I mentioned in the first chapter, there is no growth or success without some pain and risk-taking. We are all relational persons. Do not let your studies cheat you out of being fully human.

On the Outside

Cultivate your interests outside of school. Many careers are born, not from formal education, but from hobbies or extracurricular activities like photography, journalism, sports, student government, etc. Engaging in these activities will help you develop areas of your life that are often go unchallenged traditional school settings. An added bonus is that such activities make you a more interesting person.

One hobby that I had in high school and part of college was training my female raccoon, Hermie. I know that Hermie does not sound like a female raccoon's name, but the pet shop's owner did not take biology in high school. Hermie taught me many invaluable lessons. First, she taught me the art of diplomacy. One day I came home and found my mother and Hermie in a major skirmish. It seemed that

Hermie had decided it would be great fun to "TP" my mother's bathroom, turn on all the faucets, and play in the toilet bowl. In addition, she continually flushed the toilet, which lowered the water pressure throughout the neighborhood. When my dad got home, my mother declared that it was either her or the raccoon, that they both could not live in the same house! Dad did not help matters by hesitating before he answered her. Believe me, I had to make major concessions to keep Hermie's skin off of someone else's head!

Another lesson that Hermie taught me was about the pain of parenthood. I raised her since she was six weeks old and had tried to teach her the right way to live. To my shock and pain, however, I discovered that she had gotten pregnant by some Don Juan coon who ran wild in the mountains nearby. I was devastated. How could I have raised a tramp? I had given her my life and my love, and look what she had done to me. But, she did teach me many practical and enjoyable lessons. She became a very important part of my life and helped my individual growth. Cultivating outside interests is cultivating yourself!

Developing all parts of yourself is about learning how to become a whole person. By taking care of your body, establishing nurturing relationships, and cultivating outside interests, you will enhance your total education. Never forget that you are much more than a student. A major purpose of this book is to help you become a more efficient student, so that you will have more time to develop other, equally important aspects of your life. This is the pretty bow on the present!

Sowing Seeds

Jesus told this parable: "A farmer went out to sow his seed. As he was scattering the seed, some fell along the path. It was trampled on, and the birds of the air ate it up. Some fell on rock. When it came up, the plants withered because they had no way to put down strong roots. Other seed fell among thorns, which grew up with and choked the new plants. Still other seed fell on good soil. It came up and yielded a crop a hundred times more than what was sown."

Time and effort—your seeds—are not the deciding factors on how well you do in school. You all know many students who study constantly, yet have no grasp of the information or do poorly on their exams. Conversely, you know students who get A's in their classes, regardless of the amount of sleep they get or how many breaks they take. The yield of the harvest from your studies will depend on the quality of the seeds and the way they are planted. Reviewing the major points of this book) will help you cultivate the soil of you mind.

"The Big Picture" *The Secrets of Successful Students*

1. Changing bad study habits and patterns involves being motivated to change, actually deciding to change, having the right attitude and tools for change, persevering to develop new ways, and setting yourself up to win.

2. Preparation is paramount to accomplishment. Start at the beginning of the beginning to lay a solid foundation of knowledge.

3. Study with a purpose. Know what you want to accomplish, what you have studied, and what still remains to be learned.

4. The "big picture" is what you will remember and your key to understanding the details. Start with generalities and work toward specifics.

5. Develop the discipline of organizing your time, your resources, and most of all, yourself. Use a systematic approach to your classes and be realistic in the time and energy you plan to devote to them.

6. Use the resources available to you. Read the syllabus and foundational material in your texts. Obtain review books and old tests. Glean all you can from your teachers and other students.

7. Approach your classes with a conscientious attitude in the beginning of the course, planning to do your best to establish a foundation and enhance your self-confidence.

8. Try different study methods to see what works best for you in different situations. Study in defined units with frequent review, and always try to apply what you learn.

9. Go to class. It is the basic tool for education. To profit most from lectures, be prepared for them. Read ahead to familiarize yourself with the material.

10. Listening in class involves hearing, processing, acknowledging, reacting to, and assimilating the material.

11. When taking notes, take your cues from the lecturer. Remember, notes are the basis for most exams, so a good set of notes is imperative! Rewrite them after class in order to complete and get more exposure to them.

12. Memory works best when you use association techniques. Understand the material before you attempt to memorize it, then use memory aids to develop association.

13. Learn to study with a partner. This will help you to break the monotony of studying

alone, help you to clarify question areas, give you another perspective on the important points, and give you someone to help you review for exams.

14. Prepare for exams by budgeting your study time, studying in units, and engaging in periodic overall reviews. Make sure you have a complete set of lecture notes, makeup your own test questions, and create a "big picture fact sheet."

15. Find out about the exam beforehand. Use old tests to see how the professor asks questions and what material he or she has deemed important in the past.

16. Cram to review, not for first-time exposure to the material.

17. Reviewing material right before a test increases your short-term memory and therefore your performance on the test.

18. During an exam, read the instructions carefully, answer the questions that you know first, take questions at their face value, and fight the tendency to finish quickly.

19. Learn from exams by reviewing them right after the test and questioning the professor if you disagree with him or her on the validity of certain questions or answers.

20. When writing a paper or a speech, schedule your time, choose a narrow topic, research it well, make an outline, discuss your ideas, and then write and revise your work.

21. Strategies for becoming an effective speaker involve believing in your topic, writing a good speech, and then practicing and delivering it with enthusiasm.

22. Finally, develop other areas of your life. Your education in life involves much more than just school can offer.

One final suggestion for a first-rate education is to help other students. When you excel in a class, be willing to tutor those who are struggling. I have spent many hours tutoring other students, and the harvest I have reaped for my efforts was invariably greater than that sown. Every time you teach something, it helps engrave that information deeper into you parietal lobe. For one neuroanatomy mid-term exam, I spent more than fifteen hours working with two students who were having trouble in the class. When it was over, I not only had the satisfaction of knowing I had helped two friends pass a tough exam, but I also had the pleasure of writing a perfect exam myself. You will reap what you sow, so use your talents and resources in the most productive ways possible.

Directing Your Pain

Anything worthwhile takes work, sweat, and even pain. Improving your skills as a student is no exception. If you direct your efforts, however, you can use the pain to develop a system of study that will save you time and improve your grades, and that is the bottom line of this book.

This whole process can be compared to the athlete's heart rate. When an athlete is out of condition, the heart pumps at a much faster rate than when the body is in shape. So when a person's body is well tuned, the heart works less to produce the same or increased amounts of circulated blood. Likewise, when your study skills are polished, you will spend less time getting better grades and learning more.

ABOUT THE AUTHOR

DANIEL G. AMEN, M.D. IS AN INTERNATIONALLY recognized expert in brain imaging and child, adolescent and adult psychiatry.

A Distinguished Fellow of the American Psychiatric Association, Dr. Amen pioneered the use of brain SPECT imaging in clinical psychiatric practice. Dr. Amen is the author of numerous peer-reviewed journal and popular articles, more than 20 books, and a growing number of audio and video programs. His *New York Times* bestseller, *Change Your Brain, Change Your Life*, is available in 12 languages. Dr. Amen frequently appears on national and local television and radio.

Amen Clinics, Inc.

Amen Clinics, Inc. was established in 1989 by Daniel G. Amen, MD. They specialize in innovative diagnosis and treatment planning for a wide variety of behavioral, learning, and emotional problems for children, teenagers and adults. The Clinics have an international reputation for evaluating brain-behavior problems, such as of attention deficit disorder (ADD), depression, anxiety, school failure, brain trauma, obsessive-compulsive disorders, aggressiveness, cognitive decline, and brain toxicity from drugs or alcohol. Brain SPECT imaging is performed in the Clinics. Amen Clinics, Inc. has the world's largest database of brain scans for behavioral problems in the world.

www.amenclinics.com